WE GO EAT

A Mixed Plate From Hawai'i's Food Culture

Edited by Susan Yim

Published by the Hawai'i Council for the Humanities

WE GO EAT
A Mixed Plate From Hawai'i's Food Culture

Published by

Hawai'i Council for the Humanities
3599 Wai'alae Avenue, Suite 23
Honolulu, Hawai'i 96816
Phone: (808) 732-5402
Fac: (808) 732-5432
Neighbor Islands: 1-800-HCH-1301
E-mail: info@hihumanities.org
Web site: www.hihumanities.org

Library of Congress Control Number: 2008928338
ISBN: 978-0-615-20962-3

Edited by Susan Yim
Design: Kennedy & Preiss Graphic Design

Contents

Preface

Holo i'a ka papa, kau 'ia e ka manu.
("When the shoals are full of fish, birds gather over them")
*Where there is food, people gather.**

A lot happens when we come together and share our meals. Gatherings, inherently rich in cultural and social traditions, serve what we have come to see as our common fare, with its unique flavors, surprising combinations, and inimitable style. Nothing brings us together so readily or is as connected to our lives as food. Each morsel that we consume or desire tweaks our memories and imaginations as well as our taste buds. As the Zen poet Ryokan said, "In this one bowl, there is rice from a thousand households."

For this anthology, the Hawai'i Council for the Humanities (HCH) collects a "mixed plate" of stories, commentaries, evocations, poetry, art, and oral histories from Hawai'i's rich heritage of food traditions, a metaphor discussed more fully by historian Loretta Pang in her introduction. Several selections focus on the ethics of food and our essential connection to the land here in Hawai'i and globally, with watchwords like self-sufficiency, ag-friendly environments, and local markets. Davianna Pōmaika'i McGregor, for example, writes about kua'āina beliefs, customs, and practices intimately conscious of the land and its natural resources in places relatively isolated from the forces of local economic history.

Another Hawaiian proverb illustrates this well: *He ali'i ka 'āina; he kauwā ke kanaka* ("the land is a chief, man is its servant")*. Mindful farming and its local economy can lead directly to better nutrition and even to better flavor. Still, stories about cooking and eating, as we shall see, must always be told in their

---

* From *'Ōlelo No'eau: Hawaiian Proverbs & Poetical Sayings* by Mary Kawena Pukui, Bishop Museum Press 1983.

1

own ways. We are what we eat, but also where we eat, how we eat, and with whom we eat, and perhaps even why we eat — the "kim chee test" that poet Joseph Stanton shares here is not the only test we have to pass.

The appetizer for this book came when HCH invited a group of local community and educational partners to join us in touring a Smithsonian Institute *Museum on Main Street* exhibition called "Key Ingredients: America by Food." Four sites — Kapiʻolani Community College, Kapolei Public Library, Lyman House Museum, in association with Hawaiʻi Community College, and Maui Community College — came to host the exhibit along with a companion historical display on one hundred years of food in Hawaiʻi. With assistance from HCH, the National Endowment for the Humanities, Atherton Family Foundation, and the Samuel N. and Mary Castle Foundation, the culinary arts and the humanities programs of Kapiʻolani Community College created a local history display and premiered the exhibit tour of "Key Ingredients" in June 2008.

The Hawaiʻi Council for the Humanities wishes to especially acknowledge and thank principal humanities scholar Loretta Pang, project manager Kim Schauman, editor Susan Yim, design and publishing consultant Marlene Kennedy from Kennedy & Preiss Graphic Design, Grant Kagimoto from Cane Haul Road for the cover art and illustrations, and the editorial committee for *We Go Eat: A Mixed Plate From Hawaiʻi's Food Culture* — Warren Nishimoto, Craig Howes, George Tanabe, Loretta Pang, Susan Yim, Bob Buss and Kim Schauman. Finally, HCH is grateful to the National Endowment for the Humanities and its director Bruce Cole, whose "We the People" initiative provided the core funding support for this publication.

Bob Buss
Executive Director
Hawaiʻi Council for the Humanities

Introduction

Loretta O.Q. Pang

"We go eat" is a statement, an invitation, an inclusion of folks within earshot. It expresses the food experience in Hawai'i in language drawn from local life. As people from many ethnic groups arrived and joined the Native Hawaiian host culture, the island community found ways to communicate using basic English sentence structure, often enriched with words from other languages, and meant to carry an idea directly. When "we go eat," we announce what we are going to do and invite others to join us, for eating is most satisfying when done together. We also have learned that sharing what we eat — many flavors, separate but served on one dish — extends the pleasure. This "mixed plate" tells a story of Hawai'i's food culture.

Hawai'i's food culture *is* a "mixed plate" that calls to mind layers of history and social interactions, foodstuffs both native and introduced from afar, and ethnic flavors and textures that capture the imagination and please the taste buds. More than just a delicious take-out order with ample portions, our "mixed plate" describes a "local style" of eating, sharing, and remembering in a unique island community.

The articles in this volume reflect many themes that intertwine in Hawai'i's food culture: the physical place, its products, and resulting lifestyles; the social and economic history of Hawai'i's people; ethnic diversity and reflections about food; issues of "local" identity, authentic or created; and a rich trove of memories, personal and shared, that identify life in these islands.

The earliest settlers in Hawai'i brought plants and animals that became basic food resources in the islands. Later immigrants adapted to the environment and introduced other foods, such as rice, whetting the appetite for new tastes as well. In the oral history of Nelson Ah Hoy Chun ("Nature's Work"), we meet a taro farmer, the son of immigrants from China who had grown rice in historic Waipi'o valley of the island of Hawai'i. Chun describes the farmer's respect for the forces of nature, the hard labor, and his personal satisfaction in cultivating the land. The joy of working the land continues to appeal, as we see in June Watanabe's "A Duck, Duck Here" about a city-dweller-turned-duck-farmer.

Some foods introduced into Hawai'i have become so much a part of island life that a season without them is almost unimaginable. One example is the mango, originally from India, whose abundant fruit, when shared, helps to cement neighborly relations. John Wythe White's "Unstill Life with Mangos" suggests the joys and strains of coping with this bounty. Another fruit became the basis of a major processing industry, whose fields and canneries provided a rite-of-passage work experience for generations of youth in Hawai'i. Cynthia Oi's "Summers on the Line: The Pineapple Cannery Experience" is a biographical account of summers spent working in a pineapple cannery, one of the few seasonal jobs available to teenagers before the demise of this industry in Hawai'i. Juliet S. Kono's poem "My Mother's Sugar Loaves" describes the challenge of growing this fruit on a smaller, more personal scale, and the memories they evoke in the plantation communities where neighbors shared their hard times and sweet.

The divide between urban and rural, privileged or not, in what foods people ate and how they prepared them was evident from early on. In "Hawai'i's First Celebrity Chef," Bob Dye recounts the story of the colorful Baron Robert von Oehlhoffen, King David Kalakaua's master of French cuisine, who helped launch Hawai'i's tourism industry in the 1870s. The royal household, the wealthy, and the well-connected enjoyed menus that reflected continental European and American cuisine of the era. As Willa Tanabe reveals in "By the Book: Cookbooks in Hawai'i," social class and ethnicity were still evident, but cookbooks compiled in Hawai'i from the nineteenth century up to the present increasingly have reflected the islands' cultural and ethnic diversity in ingredients and food preparations.

Nineteenth century plantation agriculture opened the islands to an influx of immigrant labor; the population and economy of Hawai'i continued to grow rapidly in the twentieth century, a consequence of post-World War II development, air transportation, changes in U.S. immigration policies, effects of statehood, and population shifts occurring throughout the world. Pride and pleasure in maintaining ethnic traditions and their special foods survived, even as the plantation lifestyle gradually declined. Cultural festivities have extended beyond their immediate population, to be shared with participants from the broader community. In her article "The Vietnamese New Year, a Time of Symbolism, Celebration, and Plenty," Betty Shimabukuro describes the symbolism and foods for the lunar new year and provides traditional recipes. Ethnic foods and activities live on in other ways: Amalia Bueno relates with gusto in her story "The Chicharon Widows," the preparation of chicharon, a food modified to suit different tastes, that these widows sell at a culture-specific sporting event.

The tendency to borrow and share foods across cultural and other boundaries has produced what residents describe as a "local style." An example might be a dish flavored for one ethnic palate which evolves into a meal blending the flavors of several groups. Peter Adler's appreciation for ox tail soup in "A Broth of Islands" describes one such pleasurable result. At the other end of the spectrum might be a dish that people relish and commonly attribute to native origin, but which is a modern creation owned by no one group but embraced by all. Kristin M. McAndrews discusses this phenomenon in "Poke: A Recent Culinary Tradition."

How to describe, define, and parse "local style" components is a brow-knitting experience, perhaps most cheerfully accessed through humor, as Lee A. Tonouchi does in "Da Zippy's Zip Pac Personality Test" and as Lee Cataluna bemoans in the recurring appearance of one common fast-food take-out source, Zippy's, in the life of "Cheryl Moana Marie Sakata." Or maybe "local style" is the fabrication of an overheated imagination with marketing potential, as described in Lee Siegel's account of images of Hawai'i conjured up by Don the Beachcomber's evocation in "Pupus of the Gods: On Hawaiian Cuisine in America During the Cold War." What is certain is that there is now a market for tastes and textures from Hawai'i. George Tanabe's analysis of "Lettuce and Laulau" explores the distribution of foods imported into Hawai'i, and more recently, the "Laulau Effect" of rising demand on the U.S. Mainland for local food products from Hawai'i.

However, the diversity of foods introduced to Hawai'i through the centuries, adaptations and fusions of tastes and preparations across cultural boundaries, and imaginative uses of key ingredients stir uneasy feelings about authenticity: What is "local food" and where is its soul? Kaui Philpotts set forth to find out. She describes her quest and conclusion in "On the Road: In Search of Good, Simple Local Food." At the end, Philpotts found her answer in an abiding spirit of aloha and in herself. Thelma Chang found an answer in the immediate kinship that folks from Hawai'i experience when they share a helping of SPAM, the touchstone for cultural bonding when away from the islands, that she describes in "SPAM I Am." There is soul in the shared experience. In his poem "Chinese Hot Pot," Wing Tek Lum evokes this sense of community in sharing a common chafing dish, whose flavors from discrete ingredients blend into a sweet broth savored at the end of the meal.

In teasing out qualities brought about by changes in Hawai'i's food culture over recent decades, Joan Namkoong concludes that "The Dishes Have Evolved, the Flavors Are Still the Same." And what might these flavors be? The answers are diverse. Most tangible are the use of familiar ingredients in novel combinations and styles of preparation, such as Hawai'i Regional Cuisine. Perhaps the "local style" encourages a willingness to see and understand through the eyes of other ethnic traditions, which allows the thoughtful eater in Hawai'i to connect with the rest of humanity. In "Taking Her to the Open Market," Wing Tek Lum reflects on visiting Honolulu's Chinatown with his wife and realizing through her observations that our Western standards of "freshness" in food collide with Asian perceptions. The openness and curiosity in seeking out other food experiences that David Choo describes in "Chewing the Fat" is an example of this facet of Hawai'i's food culture.

The location of the Hawaiian Islands in the Pacific Ocean has affected our ways of eating, sharing, and remembering. Hawai'i's people have fashioned a rich "local style" drawing values from the heritage of the Native Hawaiian host culture and from cultural traditions around the globe. This is a lifestyle which cherishes the past while respecting change, and which celebrates diversity while promoting a sense of community. In her poem "Easter: Wahiawā, 1959," Cathy Song shares her appreciation for the generations that helped create this unique lifestyle for their descendants. One aspect of the immigrant experience was the strong reliance on family, a practical need that echoed the importance of family in the home countries left behind. Eugene Kaneshiro credits his family's multi-generational solidarity in building a successful restaurant business in "The Columbia Inn Story: 'We Are Still Family.'" The melding of food — identifiable "local food" such as poke and SPAM musubi, for example — and social relations (school friends beyond family) continue to reinforce what is special in the "local style." Catherine E. Toth describes the pleasures of both in "Food and Friends." This feast of taste and spirit that is Hawai'i's "local style" finds expression in the visual arts as well. Victoria Gail-White describes the inspiration that artists draw from this unique relationship between art and food history in Hawai'i — the visual is a part of the whole.

We Go Eat: A Mixed Plate From Hawai'i's Food Culture invites you to explore the tastes, textures, and soul of Hawai'i's "mixed plate" and to savor the richness of history, experiences, and memory that are found — discrete but combined — on one platter. Enjoy!

On the Road: In Search of Good, Simple Local Food

Kaui Philpotts

I live in the new Hawai'i. The one with million-dollar houses along once modest streets and multi-million-dollar resorts on every stretch of white-sand beach. The Hawai'i with seared 'ahi tuna and mango salsa on every restaurant plate. I buy local arugula on Saturdays at the farmer's market and toss it with slices of papaya and lime vinaigrette.

This is not the Hawai'i I grew up in. I spent my earliest years on a sugar plantation on Maui, where, on nights with a full moon, I'd climb out my bedroom window and lie on the coarse elephant grass near the avocado tree to watch the moon and clouds collide. I didn't eat "Pacific Rim" cuisine. I ate fried rice — leftover rice cooked in a huge cast-iron skillet with bits of fried egg, SPAM, green onion, and ginger — prepared for us kids in the afternoon by Dolores, a teenager from the detention home in Wailuku. My mother brought her home to live with us one day and help with the chores. We loved her shamelessly.

We ate impromptu picnics of fried shoyu chicken neatly wrapped in waxed paper and musubi — perfect triangles of rice with a salty red ume in the middle. My friend Lei and I sat on the steps of the old VFW Hall in Wailuku after hula class chatting and happy with our meal.

I ate tripe stew and day-old poi, saimin with bright pink fishcake, plate lunches of curry beef stew and fried veal cutlets. We gobbled down greasy malassadas from brown paper bags while they were still hot, licking the sweet sugar from our fingers. I ate SPAM, for heaven's sake, with rice and eggs for breakfast.

Local food, as opposed to Hawaiian food, is one of the original fusion cuisines. It's home cooking introduced by immigrant laborers and their families from China, Japan, Korea, the Philippines, Puerto Rico, Madeira, and the Azores. These people came to Hawai'i in the late nineteenth and early twentieth centuries to work in sugar cane and pineapple plantations. Their blend of foods, filled with exotic flavors and whatever ingredients they could muster up here, is modest and down-home.

Somewhere in the years since childhood, my diet changed. I gave up the tasty saltiness and fat of the dishes I'd loved for a more sensible way of eating, lighter and healthier. And when I started working as a food writer, I found myself sampling sophisticated restaurant cooking, traditional haute cuisine at first, and then food that was more innovative and contemporary. I ate well, but somewhere along the way I had lost touch with real local food. When that happened, I lost some vital part of who I was. That is, until a national magazine called insisting they wanted a story on "real Hawaiian food."

I began to rediscover my love of local food by climbing on a plane in Honolulu and heading for the Big Island. A short way outside of Hilo on the Hāmākua Coast I descended into Waipiʻo Valley, narrow, deep, and filled with mystery and legend. Even in a four-wheel-drive Jeep, the rugged terrain made it seem I was traveling back in time. The valley is its own tiny ecosystem, rich in flora, irrigated by freshwater streams and waterfalls, fragrant with scents of wild ginger, ripe guavas, fresh rain. Inhabited for centuries by Native Hawaiians and long a center of traditional agriculture, it is said to be home to a dense population of spirits.

I was with John Vincent, a Native Hawaiian raised in the valley, who worked hard as a young man planting and pulling taro from the watery patches for sale in town. Vincent lives nearby and works as a maintenance engineer at a luxury resort on the Kohala Coast. On the side, Vincent supplies taro and other food products from the valley to hotels and restaurants. We drive through the damp, dense jungle growth to meet up with 66-year-old Ted Kaʻaekuahiwi, another farmer who in his youth transported the taro out of the valley on mules. Retired now from his job with the state, Kaʻaekuahiwi says he finds everything he needs to survive in this valley — taro, lotus root, edible pohole ferns, wild watercress, freshwater ʻōpae, limu, ʻopihi, and fish. The afternoon with him is a glimpse into an older Hawaiʻi.

On the way back up out of the valley later in the day, Vincent points out the wild guava, pale green kukui trees, medicinal noni, and ʻōlena plants. He stops to pick stalks of white ginger. "Here, to freshen your room," he says.

It's raining now as we speed along the coastal highway. Just off the highway is a Hāmākua coast landmark, Tex's Drive Inn, known for its warm, hearty Portuguese soup and malassadas. We pull into the parking lot and walk up to the takeout window for a taste of both. Sitting nearby are four old men, obviously plantation retirees, shooting the bull, grasping Styrofoam cups of coffee, and observing everyone who walks by. Back again on the road, our hunger satisfied, we head for my hotel on the Kohala Coast for hot showers and a stiff drink.

Up early the next day I work my way down to Amy Ferguson's kitchen at the Ritz Carlton Mauna Lani. Amy may produce sophisticated fusion food for hotel guests, but she loves local food. Amy has taken what she has learned since coming to Hawai'i and incorporated it into her hotel cuisine — red mullet with lemongrass sauce, lomi salmon with taro chips, onaga stuffed with lop cheong steamed in ti leaves. Amy loves cooking with ti leaves.

"It's Hawaiian aluminum foil," she says. She takes the taro her friend John Vincent brings her, washes, peels, and steams it before grating it like a potato and mixing it with fresh 'ahi, green onions, cilantro, lemon juice, salt, and egg. She makes the mixture into patties, fries it crisp in hot oil and serves it. It's fresh and delicious. Hardly the local food I grew up with, but good all the same.

The next day I hop on another plane for an inter-island flight to Kahului. As we fly over the island I can see how it's changed. The sea of green, waving sugar cane which once blanketed the central valley, is fighting for survival as housing tracts and golf courses spring up everywhere.

The magazine wanted me to go to Kula in upcountry Maui to meet with a group of church women who bake and sell loaves of Portuguese sweet bread — 200 to 300 a day twice a week — to raise money to restore their church's altar. The aroma in the bake shop is tantalizing and the ladies happy to see me and get the word out about their bread.

The Holy Ghost Church was built in 1894 by Portuguese laborers who preferred the cooler uplands. The parish has of late discovered that their altar is something special and raised thousands of dollars to bring European restorers to Maui to bring it back to its former glory.

My arms filled with loaves of warm bread, I get back in my car and head down the mountain deciding to drop in at Komoda Bakery in Makawao for their famous cream puffs. You never know if Komoda will be open, as they seem to take off at a moment's notice and shut down the store altogether. The cream puffs are gone by noon on most days and today is no different. I opt for a bag of macadamia nut shortbread cookies cut into the shape of hearts.

At the next gas station I stop and grab some boiled peanuts and a musubi made with fried rice and teriyaki chicken. Oh, if only they still sold the jewel-colored bottles of soda from Star Ice & Soda Works. I haven't seen those frosty six-ounce bottles in years — orange, strawberry, vanilla cream, green river, and root beer.

Back in my hotel on the west side of the island, I realize that I should be sick of food by now. But I'm not. I've just been nibbling here and there, enough to enjoy the tastes again without filling up. The magazine story and my own private food journey continue island by island all week long.

Back in Honolulu I begin to reflect on the past few days. When I returned to Hawai'i from college in the early 1960s, I found the place I grew up in changing at an alarming rate. Cement trucks and cranes had replaced cane haulers and pineapple trucks. Those pesky kiawe trees on the beach, with thorns so deadly they poked right through your rubber slippers, were now being pruned and trimmed to beautifully frame a brilliant sunset for tourists. I had in the years since embraced the changes and even thrived. Only now and then did I stop for a moment to mourn the place where I grew up.

What my excursion in search of that magazine story had shown me was that some of the most wonderful things about Hawai'i hadn't changed at all. It showed me that in small ways, and in small pockets of places, island hospitality and diversity still existed. The true spirit of aloha, extended by unpretentious people with generous hearts still thrived. Humble food, odd food, heritage dishes that morphed into something typically local and regional were alive and well. I'd just stopped looking for it.

I had gone out on an assignment in search of good, simple local food and had found my way back to myself.

Kaui Philpotts is a freelance writer whose books include island cookbooks, *Hawaiian Country Tables* and *Great Chefs of Hawai'i*; tropical floral design, *Floral Traditions at the Honolulu Academy of Arts*; interior design, *Hawai'i: A Sense of Place* with Mary Philpotts McGrath; and entertaining, *Party Hawai'i*. She is a former food columnist for *The Honolulu Advertiser* and feature writer at *The Maui News*. This article was adapted from a piece published in *Saveur* magazine in 1994.

SPAM I Am

Thelma Chang

Lunch at Hawai'i public schools in the 1950s and 1960s cost a student somewhere around twenty-five cents. Even that proved to be a burden for my mother who struggled, mostly alone, to raise her children. So every other day she made SPAM sandwiches for me — the SPAM lovingly wrapped between lettuce leaves on white bread — and packed them in a brown paper bag.

I sometimes looked longingly at my classmates' school lunches, complete with an entrée (like Spanish rice or stew), canned vegetables, and a carton of milk. But my SPAM sandwiches proved not only to be sufficient, they also served as a cultural "glue" when I eventually ventured far beyond the school cafeteria.

My flight attendant career with the airlines introduced me to faraway places with strange-sounding names, people, and a life education I never imagined. And packed away in my suitcase or Los Angeles apartment: SPAM in its trademark can.

This "other world" life began with in-flight training school in Los Angeles. There, I was exposed to food and drink that were strange to me — from European cheese and fine wine to entrees with French names served on elegant china. Back then, first-class passengers who were traveling, say, from Los Angeles to Chicago, were treated to several courses of food, starting with appetizers and ending with a snifter of brandy. In-flight meals were cooked or heated on board, featuring such dishes as prime rib, lobster, Duck L'Orange and a tiny barbecued bird — I can't remember, was it squab or quail?

There we were, appearing polished and acting as if we knew exactly what we were talking about: "Madam, would you care for our *coq au vin* or lobster thermidor?" I distinctly remember one businessman soaking up the whisky. "Sir, was it for you a Johnny Walker or a Pinch?" In his drunken state, he burst out laughing and replied: "Pinch, Pinch, Pinch."

11

We took and passed the "gourmet" courses but if you asked me a question today about wine or cheese, I'd probably say, "What?" Oh, I learned soon enough to "dine" with my sophisticated, well-traveled colleagues as opposed to my usual "go eat" crowd in Hawai'i, but you know the saying, "You can take someone out of Paris, but you can't take Paris out of...." Well, this ran in reverse for me. I loved the foods of Hawai'i, including SPAM, and the way my mother packed my every-other-day school lunch.

After graduation from flight school, I found an apartment in a safe, "nice" area, but new hires generally endured a fair amount of initial financial hardship. During that time I invited a few of my flying friends for dinner and created a SPAM dish in a locale where SPAM was considered almost, well, vulgar. I dressed up the SPAM blocks with a glaze of honey, sugar, pineapple juice, and other spices I can't recall today. My Caucasian colleagues couldn't believe their eyes at first, "SPAM?"

I replied, "Hawaiian steak with my own sauce." They never blinked an eye and ate or, should I say, dined on my creation as if it were a special Thanksgiving country ham. But that's what friends are for — support, laughter, and a little bit of denial. In time we were dining at so-called hot spots in west Los Angeles, where Hollywood stars appeared occasionally. "Wow," I thought. "I've come a long way from SPAM."

However, when the Los Angeles flight scene proved tiring for me, I signed up for a stint in Southeast Asia, mainly Vietnam, under the auspices of the Military Air Command (MAC) during the height of the war. Hawai'i stopovers meant a dash to a local diner and a feast of either Portuguese sausage, SPAM, lop cheong, char siu, teriyaki beef, or the comfort of Chinese jook.

The flights to Vietnam, with stopovers in the Philippines or Okinawa, were long and filled with 165 exhausted soldiers and between eight to nine crew members. Luckily I had enough time in places like Vietnam or Thailand to taste a variety of soups and fresh noodle dishes that would become an integral part of Hawai'i's culinary scene years later.

It was a welcome break from Mainland flights, though in-flight military food at the time did not come remotely close to the *haute cuisine* served on commercial first-class journeys. Military meals ranged from breakfast pancakes with a sickeningly sweet raspberry sauce to "mystery meat" smothered in gravy, all served in tin-foil pans. I thought the reverse should have been the case — that soldiers dine on steak and lobster on fine china before they faced the brutish realities of war.

The tin-pan specials were also our designated crew meals, so I occasionally whipped out my SPAM sandwiches, lop cheong or barbequed chicken and rice and shared them with anyone who wasn't stuck up about the matter. That sharing included a soldier.

Though I never got his name, to my regret, he was a part-Hawaiian youth, perhaps nineteen years of age, sitting a few rows away from my galley and on his way to Bien Hoa, Vietnam. As I passed by his row, I noticed he hardly touched his mystery meat, instead manipulating his plastic fork around the entrée and eating the peas and carrots instead. He looked at me. It was one of those Hawai'i-to-Hawai'i moments — simply by exchanging glances we connected.

I said, "I've got some SPAM sandwiches, also lop cheong and rice." His eyes lit up. He chomped on my SPAM sandwich as if it were filet mignon. He scooped up the lop cheong and rice. The Caucasian soldier sitting next to him simply stared at the both of us: "Ya' all like that stuff, huh?"

Yeah. We do.

SPAM served as a cultural bond on yet another trip, this one to Kadena Air Force Base in Okinawa and the nearby Koza Palace Hotel. More often than not, we crashed on our beds and snored for hours after an exhausting ten-hour trip. Back then, I was known as a "Rip Van Winkle" because I could sleep for ten to twelve solid hours, while the rest of the crew managed to shop, dine, or guzzle a few during a layover. I got out frequently enough, usually hunted for a noodle stand along a narrow lane lined with bars, and consumed my dinner standing up. Once, my dinner "companion" was a horse who was hitched to a wagon outside a nightclub. We stared at each other warily.

During one Okinawa stopover, my roommate arose earlier, quietly left the room and me sleeping soundly, scrunched under a futon like a lump on the bed. The maid entered, no doubt thought the room was empty, and started to clean, humming all the while. I suddenly awoke, threw the covers off, and the maid screamed in fright, jumping skyward. "I tot nobody, I tot nobody...," she yelled.

After we both calmed down, we sat and laughed till our stomachs ached. Feeling hungry by now, I whipped out the last SPAM sandwich from my flight bag and shared it with her. She walked over to her cleaning supply box and brought out two cans of soda. We had a blast.

Today SPAM, even low-salt SPAM, will have its critics and name-calling, from "Spare Parts" to "Stuff Posing as Meat." That doesn't bother me.

SPAM served me well in a pinch long ago as it has for many other folks in Hawaiʻi. It evokes memories of my mother, a soldier, a maid, and a dinner filled with friends, laughter, and understanding.

Thelma Chang is the author of *Halekulani: A Gracious History* and the award-winning book, *ʻI Can Never Forget': Men of the 100th/442nd*.

A Broth of Islands

Peter S. Adler

Dr. Robert Putnam, a distinguished professor of international affairs at Harvard University, has an interesting theory. In a broad ranging inquiry into the decline of civic engagement and social capital in America, he has found that while more people than ever are going bowling, organized bowling has declined significantly. He thinks that individualized activities like this are a symptom of the deteriorating fabric of community. Americans, he argues in a book of the same title, are "bowling alone."

Insightful as his observation may be, Putnam has obviously never visited the Kamehameha Bowling Alley in Honolulu. If he had, his theory might have taken a different trajectory. He would inevitably have seen that social bowling springs eternal in the local soul. Nestled into the Kalihi neighborhood in Honolulu's urban core, Kamehameha Bowl, known more colloquially as "Kam Bowl," has more than twenty lanes that clatter, smack, and thunk with the sound of flying pins and gutter balls morning, noon, and night. Most of the bowlers who come to Kam Bowl are regulars and they have been enjoyably hurling gutter balls down in clubs and leagues for years.

Bowling, however, is slightly incidental to our mission. As it happens, the coffee shop inside the Kamehameha Bowling Alley is famous for its ox tail soup and Louie Chang and I have come here with the sole goal of having some. Ox tail soup is special stuff. Other hole-in-the-wall eateries serve it, but Kam Bowl's is widely regarded as the best. If you don't believe me, do your own survey. Ask Honolulu people where they go for this little gem and you will inevitably hear about the College Walk Inn, Wisteria, and Liberty Grill. So too King's Café, Masa's, Columbia Inn, the Fremont Hotel in Las Vegas where a lot of local people go to gamble, and — one day a week and at lunch time only — at the cafeteria in the Board of Water Supply Building kitty-corner from the State Capitol. Invariably, Kam Bowl's name rises to the top of the list.

It is also a cultural inter-tidal zone with a common bovine denominator. Each day a small herd of cows contributes its collective posterior anatomy to the cause. Each day, between 7 a.m. and 11 p.m., Kam Bowl's cooks stir a quarter ton of these tails into giant vats of broth. Each day a dozen waitresses shuttle back and forth from the kitchen to the dining area taking and bringing orders and chatting with customers. And each day nearly a thousand local residents, all differing by age, class, gender, ethnicity, and body morphology, troop into Kam Bowl to ooh and ah over this delectable stuff.

Louie, my navigator and chief adviser and counselor on this (and many other matters), is an esteemed colleague, a neighbor, and one of my closest friends. A quiet, soft-spoken, and exceedingly competent attorney, he takes serious interest in food and cookery. Moreover, he is extremely competent in these matters. Some of this is careful research. He explores all manner of little hidey-hole restaurants around town, reads widely about the foods he gets interested in, then tests them at home. Some of it, however, has to be his Chinese heritage. I tend not to hold many stereotypes about people but I own up to two: all Chinese are outstanding ping-pong players and they are all fixated on eating.

Under Lou's instructive and supervisory eye, this has led to some amazing culinary adventures. Over the last few years on work-related trips to America, we intentionally undertook a quest to find the world's best key lime pie. Excellent candidates have been discovered near Dupont Circle in D.C. and at a rib joint we stumbled onto by accident near Cape Canaveral where the astronauts hang out. In Baltimore, we intentionally hunted down and then relished the most succulent soft-shelled crabs on the planet. And in the dark, alien territory of Los Angeles, we traversed hostile freeways and dangerous neighborhoods to find titanic burritos that Lou had caught wind of from a friend of a friend.

Now, it is ox tail soup which tends to be humble, underrated, and not well appreciated by people with big city taste buds. Most likely it is the idea of eating the stern end of an ox. What New Yorkers, Miamians, and Chicagoans don't know, of course, is that ox tail soup is a delicacy, a local comfort food that mixes subtle flavors, ancient memories, powerful condiments, and the traditions of immigrant plantation workers from China, Japan, Korea, and the Philippines. Ox tail soup is like Hawai'i itself, a steaming broth of tropical islands, of people who all originally came from some place, of complex microclimates and subtle landscapes, of storied histories, of time-tested customs, and of peculiar dreams. All of this is stirred together in ways that attract the eye, please the palette, and soothe the soul.

Warnings are in order, of course. Anyone with low-calorie, dietary leanings will do well to avoid Kam Bowl. Yes, of course it is possible to order a side salad or fruit cup there, but no one does. Fundamentally, Kam Bowl is for meat-a-saurus kinds of people. Vegetarians and herbivores, those who philosophically refuse to eat creatures with faces, and those who are looking for vitamin supplements and grass juice energizers should just stay away. In fact, they should probably not even come to Hawai'i which has the highest per capita consumption of canned Vienna sausages and SPAM in the U.S. In Hawai'i, people tend to enjoy the meat of many different animals. We use pork and chicken as a substitute for other ingredients and we live by Redd Fox's admonition that one day all the health nuts in the world are going to feel mighty stupid lying in the hospital dying of nothing.

As it turns out, however, ox tail soup is well regarded in many climes. The Vietnamese have a recipe that is built around noodles. Germans cook veal tails into a colloidal solution of onions, diced carrots, tomatoes, bay leaves, thyme, and celery and then add a large snort of Madeira. In the English version (which no one else in the world would touch), you peel and slice turnips and throw in some ground mace, flour, and mushroom ketchup. Then, you augment the whole mess with copious amounts of ham and port wine. In Hawai'i, of course, ox tail soup has co-evolved from many different cultures. Not unlike the people who live here, it has mingled its way into something lighter and infinitely more graceful.

At the Kamehameha Bowling Alley, Lou and I settle onto two revolving stools at the end of the counter and look around. The coffee shop holds about fifty people. More people are waiting near the entrance for a table to clear. Next to us, a party of five very large men and women of mixed Asian, Polynesian, and European heritages are on their noon break. With the clack of pins in the background, they are talking and laughing and heartily spooning large amounts of soup into their mouths.

At the table next to them are three Japanese repairmen from an elevator company. All three are wearing dark green work shirts with white pocket protectors stuffed with pens, pencils, and little rulers and tools. They are working their bowls of soup with the same quiet and concentrated intensity that I hope they use when they fix the elevator in my building. Meanwhile, a whiff of cigar comes wafting in from the bowling alley. Kam Bowl may be the very last public place in the United States of America that allows smoking in general and cigars in particular. None of which is deterring the soup eaters.

Then there is the soup itself. The essence of ox tail cookery is disarmingly simple but it must be done right. You trim the excess fat off the slices of tail, wash them, then drain the water. Once they are clean and all the scum has been removed, you cover them with boiling water. If you prefer, you can brown the tails in a sauce pan first. If you are smart, you stop here, let the soup cool overnight, skim off any remaining fat, and reheat it the next morning. You add crushed ginger and garlic and maybe some mustard cabbage. Maybe some green onions, dried mushrooms, or pieces of squash. For flavor, you add dried tangerine peel, salt, pepper, Ajinomoto or star anise. Then you invite your friends and neighbors over (including Grandma Arizumi from across the street who used to run a restaurant in the neighborhood and who takes special pride in her own version). Then you eat.

At the counter, two gents sitting immediately to the left of Louie are stirring their soup and quietly debating the merits of their new cars, respectively, a Honda and a Toyota. They have their aloha shirts tucked into their crisply pressed pants and look like downtown guys, most likely bankers or insurance agents, though they could be middle managers from the Department of Land & Natural Resources or the City & County's Motor Vehicle Bureau. Next to them, a stunning and elegantly dressed Oriental woman is also at the counter engrossed in the half empty soup bowl in front of her.

She has a mysterious oval face with full lips and high, arching eyebrows. She is wearing a white flowered dress and several gold necklaces and bracelets. Louie and I speculate. I say she is half Chinese and half Korean. Louie says she's Filipino. Since he is chief counselor on most matters legal, epicurean, and artistic, I defer to him for the moment but continue pondering this important aesthetic question. A lot of eyes (male and female) are watching her but she pays them no mind. She is focused exclusively on the piece of ox tail delicately poised on the spoon in front of her. She is holding this with her left hand. With her right hand, she is ever so carefully and with great dexterity, picking out tasty morsels of meat with her chopsticks and popping them in her mouth.

The counter waitress sidles up and says: "What'll it be boys?" Louie, a man of few words, points to the bowls in front of the downtown gents sitting next to us and smacks his lips. Then, he gets up and takes a quick walk through the restaurant, leaving me to my own fate.

While he is gone, I return to the business of ethnographic research on the sartorially splendid oval-faced Filipino-Chinese-

Korean (or-whatever) woman dressed in white. Ever so discreetly I watch her adroitly handle the spoon, the chopsticks, the rice, and her soup. During a brief pause, she looks up at me. (Or is it past me?) I smile but she ignores me. I smile harder but she turns back to the bowl in front of her, fiercely, happily, and full of obvious soup-lust.

A few minutes later, Lou walks back with his intelligence report: all but seven people in the restaurant are having ox tail soup. Of those who aren't, several are eating cheeseburgers, one is having the chicken curry, and the rest have ordered the sliced tongue plate which is served with rice, gravy, shiitake mushrooms, and bamboo shoots. Beef tongue plate is a Friday special. Pigs feet soup is the Monday and Thursday special. No one is eating salad.

Our waitress comes back moments later with steaming bowls of soup, a small round condiment dish of shredded ginger, a side bowl of rice, chopsticks, and flat-bottomed Oriental spoons. We mix a little chili pepper water and Kikkoman Soy Sauce into the ginger, drop some rice in the soup, and dig in. Kam Bowl's coffee shop makes ox tail soup in industrial quantities but it is amazingly light and supple in its flavors.

So, idle conversation and sideways observations cease and we eat. Then we eat some more. And after a while, I'm thinking to myself: given enough pots of the right size and girth, given enough ox tails and rice, and given enough clean water to boil, we could feed all of Latin America on this stuff. In fact, if we fed a few bowls of Hawaiian ox tail soup to the leaders of Russia, America, China, the Congo, Israel, and Iraq, we would quickly have world peace (or at least a sudden outbreak of common sense). At the very least, everyone's bowling scores would improve.

Slurping our broth and gnawing on tail bones, I think of the feeding of everyday nourishment of bodies, minds, and souls. Soup of all kinds is a human essential. A thousand years ago in Europe, medieval remedy books extolled the virtues of chicken soup for its soothing and restorative powers. In India when I was in the Peace Corps and sick as a dog with a tropical fever, Mrs. Harnakar fed me chili pepper soup and it cleared the bugs out of me in a night. Life itself, we are told, emerged from a primordial soup of protein-like molecules after our planet cooled. And in Hawai'i, ox tail soup is ultimately all about the real Hawai'i.

Beyond the lei-bedecked images of Waikiki, beyond the long string of TV shows shot on location in the 50th State, beyond all of these ephemeral and ever glitzy images lies a place full of real people. If you want to participate in this, look around at the Kam Bowl and then join in as bones are sucked and consommé is slurped amidst the steady clatter of people bowling together.

Peter S. Adler is President/CEO of The Keystone Center and the author of *Beyond Paradise, Oxtail Soup for the Island Soul* and *Eye of the Storm Leadership.* "The Broth of Islands" was first published in *Oxtail Soup for the Island Soul by* Ox Bow Press in 2001.

Da Zippy's Zip Pac Personality Test

by Lee A. Tonouchi

In Hawai'i local culture, lotta communication stay non-verbal. For examples, even jus how you eat your Zippy's Zip Pac can say choke planny stuff about you. Based on my empirical kine observations I wen take a-notice dat you can tell wot kine person somebody is, based on wot their favorite ting stay insai da Zippy's Zip Pac. Fo' reals. But da trick is, you gotta figgah out which of da tings is da person's fav-o-rite ting.

Usually you ask people wot their favorite ting is, dey going waver. Cuz all da choices insai da Zip Pac stay so onolicious. If you ask 'em, people going say oh, depends on their mood or dey no mo' one favorite. But das all bulai, brah. Dey get. Go try watch 'em. Lotta times you can tell. Of course, da dead giveaway is if dey do one substitution. Like if dey wen sub one extra fried chicken instead of da fish, den you know chicken gotta be their broke da mout favorite.

People planny times gravitate to their favorite ting first, but I found out no always work if you jus watch wot dey eat first. You gotta figgah out wot kine eater da person you observing is. If da person you observing is one small eater, den it's true, lotta times dey eat their favorite ting first, cuz dey know dey might not pau da whole bento so dey gotta bring home da rest. If your person get big appetite, and you know dey can put da whole ting away, den chances is dey probably going save their favorite ting for last. Da only exception to dat is if da big eater stay supah hungry — supah hungry big eaters jus go on instinct so dey going start inhaling their food, probably going wit favorite ting first. Meejum size eaters you jus gotta try guess 'em, whichevah ting dey eat all of, den das probably their favorite.

Da following test stay intended for be used fo' fun kine purposes only. Dis test no stay endorsed by our state government, by Zippy's, or even by me. So if no come out, no be all blaming. I said da test not scientific and wuz jus based on wot I wen observe.

So I warning you now no get huhu if come out wrong. Below get da seven items insai da Zip Pac and their probable correlating personality types. Go try test 'em out on yourself first fo' see if work. Which ting is your favorite?

Fish — Practical. For those who dunno, da fish dey put is hoki; used to be mahi before. Whichevah da fish, you like da fish da most cuz you value da skills needed for catch da fish. Whether it be cooking, fixing cars, carpentry, wotevahs, you raddah learn how do someting yourself than pay somebody for do 'em for you, even if it means being one brokechanic sometimes. Even if you yourself is not one practical person, you still value those skill sets and chances is das da kine mate you either looking for, or get already. Get planny Hawaiian proverbs dat attest to da importance of da fisherman in da community. Likewise, you hold those kine skills and knowledges in high esteem.

Teri-Beef — Patient. You recognize good teri-beef takes one long time for marinade. You can appreciate da finer tings. J'like in life, good tings come to those who wait. You's meticulous and one planner. You probably carry around one organizer or you get one fancy PDA. You get or going get one good retirement plan and you look forward to traveling when you pau work and can retire.

Fried Chicken — Independent. You one freetinker. You no care wot oddah people tink about you. Das why you no sked eat da greasy, messy fried chicken first. Da chicken da only ting in da Zip Pac dat you gotta eat wit your hand. You like for do tings your own way and da chicken provides you wit planny options. You can hemo da skin and jus eat da chicken, or you can jus eat da skin if you like, no mattahs. If you in da mood you can even suck on da bone, cuz you, you no mo' shame you.

Spam — Spontaneous. You live for da moment cuz you love Spam even if da ting get one rep for being unhealthy. Your motto in life is "chance 'em." You live for excitement and adventure. You probably not one state worker, but if you is, probably your only way for rebel against da grind of your daily routine is for eat Spam. Pua ting you.

Rice w/Furikake on top — Devoted. You value 'ohana and you very community oriented cuz in lotta Asian cultures rice symbolizes gotta stick togeddahness. You most likely involved wit service organizations dat help people, culture, and/or da environment.

Takuan — Cautious. You like for be prepared. Takuan is thought for aid digestion and it's usually eaten at da end of da meal so if you cannot wait, and gotta grine all your takuan right away, dat must mean you like for be extra prepared. Like you show up half an hour early for appointments. You always double check everyting before you go sleep — you check da door, stove, and even da faucet for make sure not dripping. Most likely you love for shop in bulk and das how come you get choke toilet papah and can goods stock up your house.

Green Decoration Ting — Naïve. Is dis anybody's favorite ting for EAT? If you chose dis one, den maybe you nevah ate one Zip Pac befo'. Cuz in all likelihood you probably not from Hawai'i cuz oddahwise you would know da ting is ony dea for make da bento look pretty. Why you wen believe some kolohe local person who played one trick on you and said you can eat dat?! Da ting not going make your breath come smell good. Das plastic, brah. No eat 'em, bumbye you going come ma-ke die dead!

"Da Pidgin Guerrilla" Lee A. Tonouchi is da co-editor of *Hybolics* magazine; writer of da award-winning book of pidgin short stories, *Da Word;* author of da pidgin essay collection, *Living Pidgin: Contemplations on Pidgin Culture;* and editor of *Da Kine Dictionary: Da Hawai'i Community Pidgin Dictionary Projeck.* At Hawai'i Pacific University, he teaches da course English 3203: Pidgin Literature.

mixed plate

with double order rice, macaroni and gravy over everything

Cheryl Moana Marie Sakata

Lee Cataluna

So I'm sitting on the bench at Zippy's waiting for my large chili cracka and thinking if I gotta' stop Foodland still yet on the way home and what was on sale at Longs this week and then it hits me:

My whole life is Zippy's, Foodland, Longs.
Zippy's, Foodland, Longs.

Sometimes, the order change little bit.
If I buying stuff like ice cream or frozen chicken, I go Foodland last.
Or if I pick up the kids, then I do my shopping first and take them Zippy's after.
But other than those variations, that's it.

Longs, Zippy's, Foodland.
Foodland, Longs, Zippy's.
Zippy's, Foodland, Longs. Zippy's, Foodland, Longs.

And I tried to think when my life wasn't Zippy's, Foodland, Longs.
Before I had kids,
before I got married,
before I got married again.

Small kid time, same thing.
Instead of Zippy's, we went Diners and instead of Foodland my mada had Tamashiro's down the street.
But Longs was Longs.

I think there was like this short time in-between high school and the first baby when I actually went to a real restaurant.
Not like Sizzler or Wailana, but the kind with tablecloth.
I remember thinking that it took a really long time for the food to come, but nobody else looked pissed off so I figured that's just how it is.
I guess so people who go to real restaurants have the time.
They don't have to run to Foodland and Longs after.

And as I'm sitting there, trying to think how many years of my life I've spent sitting on a bench at Zippy's waiting for my damn chili cracker, it hits me again, but this time, it's even worse.
This is my whole life.
This is the rest of my life.
Zippy's, Foodland, Longs.
Zippy's, Foodland, Longs.

When I'm an old, old lady and can hardly walk, going be the same thing:
Zippy's, Foodland, Longs,
Zippy's, Foodland, Longs.

Except, going be real early in the morning.

Lee Cataluna is a columnist for *The Honolulu Advertiser*, author and playwright and recipient of the 2004 Cades Award for Literature. Her favorite stories, fiction and non-fiction, are about ordinary people struggling to live lives of dignity and purpose. "Cheryl Moana Marie Sakata" is reprinted with permission from the book *Folks You Meet in Longs and other Stories* published by Bamboo Ridge Press in 2005.

Summers on the Line: The Pineapple Cannery Experience

Cynthia Oi

The woman, dressed in office attire, was discreet enough to wait a couple of stops before she left the seat next to mine. She slipped into the aisle past my knees, holding her neat skirt close lest it brush against me, and stood near the exit door.

I was thoroughly embarrassed, but understood why neither she nor anyone else on the bus wanted to get near. I stunk. All summer long, I stunk. So did thousands of other teen-age girls who had the good fortune of working in a pineapple cannery. I say good fortune because not everyone got a cannery job.

For the privilege of standing through shifts as long as twelve hours, six days a week for three months on the hottest days of the year, you had to have "pull." You had to know somebody who knew somebody else who could get your name on the hiring list as a "seasonal" employee.

The coveted jobs earned high school and college kids as much as $1,000 or more during summer vacation in the days when island school schedules still kept tempo with agricultural harvests. Pineapple was one of them, coming ripe in vast fields across Hawai'i just as classes let out.

The pineapple, like the artichoke or oyster, will always draw wonder about who was the first soul brave or hungry enough to eat one. It is a formidable fruit, crowned by scythes of sharp-tipped leaves, its thick skin deeply quilted in diamonds that hold small spikes at their centers.

Were it not for Henry Ginaca, pineapple might have stayed an exotic luxury, a niche product for the moneyed classes. But at the behest of grower James Dole, the clever engineer invented a namesake machine that became the life force for pineapple, spurring a crop that would become second only to sugar in the rich soil of the Hawaiian Islands.

The Ginaca capped, cored and peeled the pineapple, loosing a golden cylinder largely free of eyes and its fibrous core, and sent the sweet-acidic fruit sliding down a chute and onto a belt to a trimmer. Trimmers, armed with slim-bladed knives and gouges, cut off skin and picked out imperfections the Ginaca missed. That done, they tossed the cylinders back on the conveyer belt that ran through a slicer.

That's where I came in. I was a packer, a title clearly descriptive of the job. Along with thousands of other girls and women, I stood at a long stainless steel table putting pineapple slices into cans. As easy as that sounds, there was technique and criteria involved. Packers graded each pine, slice by slice, checking look, texture, and translucence, an indicator of higher acid and less sweetness. Imperfect or broken slices were dropped backed onto the belt. Passable fruit, called "choice," mostly from the pineapple's top, went into one set of cans, to be sold under off-brand labels. The bottom "fancy" slices, sweeter and more firm, went into another set of cans that would wear the premium label.

When a can was full, it was spun on to a chain belt to be sugared, lidded, and cooked, and eventually boxed for shipment to grocery stores across the country and the world. Packers had just a few seconds to make judgments and slap the slices into the correct cans because fruit came down the line whether you were ready for them or not. And because each packer was assigned a pine, there was no hiding a missed one.

Let too many go by or build a pile in front of you and you'd get a scolding. These were usually administered by your table's forelady, as the older women who oversaw canning were called. Distinguished by a blue band on their caps, foreladies were the noncoms of the operation, keeping an eye on production, watching for waste and poor grading. Some were maternal, gently teaching novices the tricks of the trade, correcting mistakes, helping an overwhelmed packer when necessary. There were others who yelled and even got physical, pushing packers from the line and sending them home.

I was lucky to work most seasons for Cecelia, a big-boned woman whose physical presence scared me at first. Her firm, no-nonsense attitude, however, was balanced by sympathy and patience, even for an incurably clumsy fifteen-year-old intimidated by the unfamiliar world of food production.

What a mad world it was. Though most people associate the cannery with its acrid odor, for me, the most remarkable thing was the noise. In a building that stretched as wide and as long as two or three football fields with open ceilings three stories high, scores of machines clanged and sputtered, competing with the racket of hundreds of thousands of clattering, colliding cans. Overhead, miles of chain belts ripped through looping paths while huge fans squealed in feeble attempts to cool the air. To speak to the packer next to you required putting your mouth inches from her ear. (I suspect many foreladies got raps for being mean because they had to shout to be heard.)

If pure cacophony wasn't bad enough, some executive one summer decided that since most seasonals were teenagers, pop music should be added to the din. But either by cruel design or plain cluelessness, only a single record, "Cherish," was played over and over again. After hours of repetition, day after day, the sappy song by a group called The Association became torture. To survive, I made a game of dreaming up alternative lyrics to reflect the awful tediousness of packing pine.

The job had you standing for hours, leaning over a counter in the heat and stench. Pineapple contains acid powerful enough to eat away at the soft flesh under fingernails. Bleeding was a most reliable signal for the need for new gloves and a trip to the dispensary where nurses would give out Band-Aids. They would also treat the rash the juice burned onto forearms, slathering greasy ointment up to the elbows before covering the goop with lengths of gauze that would only soak up more juice.

I packed pine for four summers, three of them with high school friends, the last — and the worst — all by myself. There was no one to share the misery of shifts that grew to twelve hours as students quit near season's end to get ready for school or enjoy a few weeks off.

There were days when I put on apron and cap as the flare of a setting sun flooded through the windows of the locker room, knowing it would be dawn when I took them off. There were days when I wished for the end of summer, but my need to earn money for college tuition kept me packing.

The last cannery shut down in 2007, ending the era of big agriculture in Hawai'i. Pineapple, like sugar, has fled the islands, finding cheaper land and wages elsewhere. Much of the red soil on O'ahu, Maui, and other islands that were striped in dark-green plantings now sprout housing developments and resorts.

The cannery building I worked in has been converted into shops and a multiplex, the surrounding land covered in big box stores. A water tank shaped like a huge pineapple, a landmark in Honolulu for decades, was taken down fifteen years ago.

But traces of the industry remain in the memories of young seasonals grown older, whose work in the cannery and fields earned money for higher education and other opportunities. I don't often eat pineapple, but when I do, its sweet-sharp notes fit perfectly with my appreciation of the fruit.

Cynthia Oi is an opinion writer and columnist at the *Honolulu Star-Bulletin*. In addition to the *Star-Bulletin*, she has worked at *USA Today* and in Connecticut for the *Hartford Courant* and *The Chronicle*. After a swim in the ocean on a hot day, she says, "A slice of pineapple (with chewy core) beats all."

My Mother's Sugar Loaves

Juliet S. Kono

My mother grows pineapples in her backyard.
What started with one plant
increased to several rows of them.
She uprooted the wing-bean vines,
Swiss chard and cherry tomatoes
to cultivate this spiny fruit.

The island she lives on
has always been noted for sugar cane.
Her father once owned acres.
In her town
anyone will tell you that it's impossible
to grow pineapples,
the climate too wet,
the fruits needing a lot of sun.
But her pineapples thrive.
Sugar loaves, she calls them.

The neighbor children
call her the "pineapple lay-day."
Friends come with sacks of papaya
or bananas to exchange.

I've heard her apologize to friends
that it's too bad they only grow in summertime.
She wishes she had more to give,
generous that she is.
"If I had more land...."
Good omiyage for friends.
Mezurashi off-island gift.

Out back and showing me her crop,
she says that people on the Big Island
had been growing the wrong thing all along.
"They should have grown pineapples."
And she sticks a new crown into the ground,
for emphasis.
She taps a fruit,
selects one for us to taste.
"This year too rainy. Might be sour."
Back in the house, she slices the pine
and pops small wedges into her mouth.

She passes a plateful of pine for me to try.
She's afraid it's too acidic.
I can't tell. I only know it's a bit
tart, but sweet.
And it's like taking a bite
into a slice of my childhood.
Some other fruit before me,
another kitchen table
where she and my grandfather
discussed an ailing crop,
the seamless edge
between poverty and paying the bills.

At night, she goes out to chase the cats
and takes a last walk in her garden.
She bends over to pull
a stray weed or two,
then straightens her back
to survey her plot of land.
Queen of the hill,
she sleeps under the smell of pine fruit
and the rustle of long, spiked leaves.
I hear her behind our doors,
this woman whose breath
rises and falls like the backyard wind,
who, at her old age,
still dreams of plantations.

Juliet S. Kono had her first poems published by Bamboo Ridge in 1982. Since then, she has continued to write poems and short stories. Her most recently published work is a children's story called, *The Bravest 'Opihi.* "My Mother's Sugar Loaves" is reprinted from *Tsunami Years* published by Bamboo Ridge Press in 1995. Kono says, "I miss my mother's pineapple and her singing in the garden."

Nā Kua'āina:
Living Hawaiian Culture

Davianna Pōmaika'i McGregor

Waipi'o Valley, circa 1931, typified a remote, small community that was predominately Native Hawaiian, and the pace of life was slower than that of people exposed to the social and economic changes that were transforming the rest of the island of Hawai'i.

Waipi'o provided its people with an abundance of natural resources for their day-to-day sustenance. They did not have to seek high-wage jobs or venture outside of the valley for this subsistence. Taro was the staple food of the Hawaiians. It was boiled or fried and eaten whole or else pounded into poi. Poi was pounded on an ongoing basis in the valley with pounders that had been fashioned by their fathers and grandfathers out of beach stones. Breadfruit, which was available on a seasonal basis, was usually cooked in the imu and pounded into poi. It was eaten by itself or mixed together with taro poi.

The leaves of the taro, especially the young lū'au or taro shoots, were cut up and boiled for greens with pork, chicken, or jerked beef. They were also gathered along the streams and in common land areas. The aquatic life of the mountain streams was the main protein source for the Hawaiians of Waipi'o in 1931. 'O'opu fish and 'ōpae or shrimp were caught in the streams and taken home, cleaned, and either salted for later consumption or cooked right away by boiling or frying with salt or shoyu. Sometimes the 'o'opu were baked in ti leaves. Freshwater shrimp were sometimes eaten raw.

David Makaoi provided a graphic description of the preparation of fish for eating: "I didn't tire of eating 'o'opu. That's one thing I found out. Could cook it and maybe roast it sometimes, or boil it. The gravy tastes nice, it's fat. It's tasty. And fry. And sometimes cook in the ti leaf too over the fire. Gives a different flavor. So, you can cook it in many ways. So, you never get tired of eating fish. So we had fish most of the time."

The people of Waipiʻo made fish traps with the ʻieʻie vine to catch ʻoʻopu and shrimp. The trap would be placed in the stream, facing a rock, and the ʻoʻopu and shrimp would be scared into the trap. During floods, the ʻoʻopu washed downstream and could be easily caught with traps placed at strategic points in the stream. In the ocean, the ʻoʻopu spawned and hatched their young, called hinana. The Hawaiians would go to the mouth of the river and scoop hinana up with the nets. Many escaped and swam upstream, where they lived in the pools deep in the back of the valley and in the stream along the muddy banks. In dry weather, the ʻoʻopu could be caught in the upper pools of the valley. Slapping the water would scare them into holes in the sides of the pool. Then one could stick a hand into the hole and gently grab the fish by the head.

Mullet found in the lower valley were usually cooked in ti leaves and fried or boiled. Pūpū and escargot-like shellfish were raised in the taro patches. They were usually left to stand for three days in a kerosene tin and then cleaned, after which they could be heated on a stone until they cracked and were either removed with a needle or sucked out. Sometimes they were boiled with garlic, black beans, and salt and then served.

Freshwater fish were plentiful in Waipiʻo. George Farm described how he once took the father of a friend to Waipiʻo Valley during the depression of 1929 and 1930. He drove by car to the top of the valley and then rode by horse down into the valley. He was very impressed with the abundance of fish:

"Lot of fish, Waipiʻo. You don't have to go hunt for it. The fish in the taro patches, fish in the ditches, fish in the streams, all over the place. And then one night when we slept there, the first night, they had big storm down there. Lot of rain. And the streams got flooded over, eh? And in the morning, about 7 o'clock, I see young children with the bucket. They running in the bushes, they pick up fish. Fill up the buckets, going home, empty and bring it back again. Filling up fish whole morning, you know. So I stopped them one time. I say, 'Say, where you get that fish from? Where you buy that fish?' 'No, no. No buy. Plenty in the bushes.' You see, that much fish in Waipiʻo Valley."

Limu or seaweed was a very important source of vitamins and minerals to the Hawaiians. They would gather it from the ocean, clean it, salt it, and eat it raw with poi. It was never cooked. The ocean provided limu kohu, limu huluhuluwaina, ʻeleʻele, lipuʻupuʻu, maneʻoneʻo, and lipaheʻe varieties of seaweed. Limu kohu, the hardest to get, also lasted the longest, two to three months, while the others usually lasted a week. Salt was not made in Waipi'o but was obtained from Kawaihae, Hawai'i, or directly from Honolulu by the Chinese storekeeper.

The valley was also rich in fruits, trees, and plants for eating and healing. It had 'ōhi'a'ai or mountain apple, papaya, banana, avocado, breadfruit, guava, and mango trees. Coffee also grew wild in the valley. It was gathered, dried, and roasted in a skillet for home use. There were also lemon trees, orange trees, coconuts, hau trees, noni fruit, 'awa, and chili peppers. Kukui trees were plentiful, and its nuts were used for garnishing food, for medicine, and to make small torches. Wauke and olonā, traditionally important for making tapa and cordage, also grew wild in the valley, although they were not actively used in 1931. Pandanus trees grew in the valley; its leaves were gathered for weaving. Even as late as 1931 women wove mats, hats, purses, handbags, and headbands from the pandanus leaves.

Wild goats in the mountains were sometimes shot for food. Both Hawaiians and Chinese owned 200 head of cattle which grazed in the valley. They were periodically slaughtered for home consumption by families in the valley. Every two months or more someone would plan to slaughter a cow and go throughout the valley to all the families to let them know. He would butcher it in the pasture, and the meat would be placed in piles on fern or water lily leaves. Everyone who wanted to buy meat would come to the site and select the piles, which sold for one dollar, two dollars, or five dollars, that they wanted to buy. The bones, which were used for soup, were given away free. They did not use a scale. People brought their own bags to take home their meat. The meat was usually salted, dried, and kept in crocks or barrels until it was ready to be eaten, because there were no iceboxes or freezers.

Aside from these occasions, meat was rarely eaten in the valley, and the nearest butcher was at the town of Honoka'a. One would have to make an order ahead of time, and he would arrange for the meat to be delivered to Kukuihaele on the specified day. David Makaoi explained why meat was not often eaten:

"Hardly any meat. 'Cause only once in awhile, when somebody kills a cow for the whole valley. Then they get to buy beef, so many pounds to take home. And salt it most of the time. And that's pipikaula (smoked beef). That's the only way to preserve it and still be nice for eating. So that's why I enjoy pipikaula, nowdays, here, because it has a good flavor."

Despite the abundance of natural resources for food, certain items — sugar, flour, salt, shoyu, rice, canned salmon, canned sardines, salt salmon, cod fish, dried shrimp, corned beef, cooking oil, matches, kerosene oil, soap, beer, wine, sake, and clothing — were purchased in stores in Waipiʻo, Kukuihaele, and Honokaʻa. The store in Waipiʻo also sold baked goods, such as bread with butter and jelly, doughnuts, and cakes, which were popular with the school children.

In general, the people of Waipiʻo only purchased the bare necessities. According to David Makaoi:

"We didn't buy too much, though, because for the rest of the things we were self-supporting. We just say, 'Why spend money? Get up and make our own.' We were independent. We didn't need much cash for things in the store. So, that's why they said, 'Why live in town? You have to buy everything with cash.' In the country, you don't need much cash."

Those Hawaiians who sold taro to the store could purchase goods on credit. Those who sold the taro to another broker or who did not sell taro had to purchase goods on a cash basis.

Fannie Hauanio Duldulao, who was born in Waipiʻo in 1911 into a Hawaiian family that raised taro in Waipiʻo, probably expressed the feelings of everyone who was born and raised there:

"Well, I love the place because I was born and raised there until I grew up — a great-grandmother today. And then the feelings of the place is actually really warm feelings ... It's a valley of aloha and then full of love. And when I was born and raised there, I had everything that I can think of without spending money. Everything was really from the land, what we raised. The valley. Like taro and everything."

This edited excerpt is from *Nā Kuaʻāina: Living Hawaiian Culture* by Davianna Pōmaikaʻi McGregor, published by the University of Hawaiʻi Press in 2007. McGregor is a professor and founding member of the Ethnic Studies Department at UH-Mānoa. She is a historian of Hawaiʻi and the Pacific.

Nature's Work

Nelson Ah Hoy Chun

A farmer has to rely on nature. That's my policy. Nature not with you, you just out of luck. One disease can sweep you clean, one flood can sweep you clean. It's just nature's work. How you going stop? It's just impossible to stop. If you lose one crop, it takes you two, three crops to get back to your feet.

You know what I mean by losing? One time, after my father and his workers harvest the rice, one flood come down, sweep 'em. After one whole day cutting, the flood takes the rice all away. What can you do? Just drop tears, that's all. Somebody asked me one time, "What if human being do that?"

I said, "I shoot that fellow down."

I realized my father was a rice farmer when I was a small kid, about six years old, when we were working in our farm together. But all that time, when you small, you don't take notice of what the parents doing.

He came down Waipi'o to start a rice farm around the late 1890s. Before that, I really don't know what he did in China. Must be he rice farmer. They get just small portion. In China hard to own plenty land, you know. You had to be rich to own plenty.

In my early days, rice farming was done by hand: planting, harvesting, everything. Plowing, you use two horses and two people managed the team. One is the driver and one holds the plow. And you have to harrow three, four times before you can break up the soil. Then you have to prepare seed beds where you want the rice seedlings to start. You try and plant in the high place where floods doesn't catch. Of course, when Waipi'o floods, our section always catch. Get real big water. So planting's really not easy work, you know. Even harvesting hard work. You start in the morning. Half an hour after that you get all soaked wet.

But the worse job when I was small was scaring away the rice birds. We built a tower from twelve to sixteen feet above the ground. It had a platform to sit down on. And get ten, fifteen lines of string, all come to the tower. You strip cloth rags — you tie on. And get the five-gallon kerosene can at the end and drop four or five kukui nut in there. Every time you pull the string, the rags going shake. The birds scared, eh. And that noise from the cans — the birds get scared, fly away.

So from morning time, as soon as dawn, you there on the platform. And you don't get your breakfast until somebody come relieve you. You go home, eat, and come back again. Pretty soon the birds go into the guava and they watch. Little by little, they try to sneak into the rice field. So you have to be wide awake and keep on shaking the can. Otherwise they be eating before you know it.

Sometimes, no matter how you try, they won't fly away. One time they got me so mad I went home, get the twelve gauge, and went try blow 'em down.

But still yet they come. They have time to fill their stomachs before they go home to nest. Just before dark you see them going. Hoo, by the thousands! In the morning you see them swooping down — airplane is not as fast.

Even after the rice was harvested and bundled up, birds used to come and eat. So I grab my net, go sneak around from behind and throw the net right over, catch 'em. One crack, 600, 700, 800 birds.

And we eat 'em! Good-eating birds, you know. But to clean 'em, ah, that's not an easy job. You de-feather, but don't skin 'em. You skin 'em, doesn't taste good because the fat on the skin. Cut the heart, throw 'em out. Cut 'em open from the back, take off the guts, wash everything. My brother, Ah Kong, was fast with his fingers. He could clean two, three; we cannot clean one. Even my mother cannot beat him. Then you face 'em down on the chopping board and just slap 'em with da kind Chinese knife. You smash the bones, they come flat.

Then you get shoyu, salt, little bit sugar, and marinate that for an hour or so. Dip that bird in egg batter and deep fry the thing. The big bone you cannot eat, but the small bones, you can chew 'em. You ever try that, boy, you won't eat any other birds.

This oral history of Nelson Ah Hoy Chun, a farmer in Waipi'o Valley on the island of Hawai'i, was recorded by Vivien Lee in 1978 by the Center for Oral History at the University of Hawai'i. It appears in *Hanahana: an Oral History Anthology of Hawai'i's Working People*, edited by Michi Kodama-Nishimoto, Warren S. Nishimoto, and Cynthia A. Oshiro, and published in 1984.

Lettuce and Laulau

George Tanabe

Iceberg lettuce gets no respect. True to its name, it tastes like water. The pale green, cabbage-looking head is the butt of jokes for its lack of flavor and class. Filmmaker John Waters calls it "the polyester of greens" in his essay, "100 Things I Hate." Nutritionists rank it low in their lists, noting that even its cousin Romaine has three and a half times the amount of vitamin K, nearly eight times more vitamin C, and ten times the level of beta carotene. Iceberg lettuce is easily overlooked, making it a perfect hiding place. A company selling a hollow plastic replica of the crisp head promotes it through its lowly reputation: "Have you ever heard anybody say, 'Oh no, somebody stole all my lettuce!' Me neither, so what better place to hide your valuables than inside an authentic looking Iceberg lettuce."

And yet this maligned vegetable has its merits, most obviously its crunch, crackly like ice, not hard and fibrous like cabbage. The word lettuce shares the same Latin root with lactic, pertaining to milk, and anyone who has cut a head of lettuce from the garden knows that the stem weeps a milky liquid. When collected and dried, the substance is known as *lactucarium,* or lettuce opium since it has mild psychotropic effects. The drug enjoyed some popularity in the late nineteenth century, fell out of use, then re-emerged in the 1970s in the counter-culture movement as a legal, mind-altering substance. Lettuce opium has trace amounts of morphine, a million times less than a standard therapeutic dosage, and some aficionados of lettuce claim that their salads give them a remarkable sense of well-being. But the poor lettuce, even as an opiate, is mocked as a "venerable fraud of a drug" in *Tyler's Honest Herbal* published in 1999.

So how did the lowliest of leafy vegetables come to dominate the world of salads as its undisputed sovereign? It is the most widely used of all greens, and the watery Iceberg has garnered a place high on the list of staple foods, even here in Hawai'i. No accounting of local foods can leave out Iceberg lettuce. Genetic breeding has a lot to do with its popularity, having produced a vegetable to resist rot and transport well, but that is only half the story. The other half is the distribution system that delivers it fresh from farm to table. The success of lettuce is attributable more to technology than taste.

"It tastes like nothing," says Ann Asakura, expressing the widely held opinion about Iceberg lettuce, the mainstay import of Ala Moana Produce, the company of which she is president. "I hate it, and I don't eat it myself." Ann's company is a mid-sized player in the produce field, and serves a wide range of clients ranging from Jack in the Box to small restaurants, mom-and-pop stores, and the Kalaupapa Settlement, a special client. Eighty percent of her products are brought in from the Mainland, lettuce heads in the thousands making up the largest percentage.

The irony of Mainland lettuce is that it can outlast locally grown Mānoa lettuce in freshness. Hawai'i is too warm to grow Iceberg and Romaine, the king and queen of shelf life, and they must be brought in from the Sacramento Valley. "It takes five days," says Ann, "for a head of lettuce to leave the California fields and appear in our local markets."

The distribution system is closely orchestrated by Ann and Vice President Randy Okabe, who orders, coordinates, consolidates, and trouble shoots shipments by sea and air. It is not easy to move fragile vegetables by the tens of thousands speedily and safely across the ocean, and distributors need to respond to constantly changing conditions.

Ala Moana Produce is a success largely because of Ann's mother, Helen Asakura, an astute business woman in a field dominated by men. She started as a clerk at Ala Moana Produce, then owned by Edward Ogawa, when she was still a high school student before the Pacific War, when River Street was a hive of vegetable wholesalers, at the center of which was Rancho, run by the Asakura family. After marrying Ray Asakura, she continued to work in the produce trade, but left it for a period of some years.

In the late 1950s, Helen returned to Ala Moana Produce, and helped Edward Ogawa set up air shipments necessitated by the 1959 dock strike. They established a separate corporation with a standardized pricing structure for the newly arrived fast food franchises, beginning with the first McDonald's in Aina Haina. She also helped develop new processing and distribution procedures to fit McDonald's special needs. In 1963, a fire completely destroyed their warehouse, except for the fire proof safe that Helen had the earlier foresight to purchase. Ala Moana Produce recovered from the fire and did well serving smaller clients and major franchises such as Wendy's, Harpo's Pizza, Jack in the Box and McDonald's, which all continued to open new outlets. In the 1980s, Helen Asakura bought the business from Ogawa, and retired only recently, turning over the management of the company to her daughter Ann.

It is easy to take for granted the people and the technology behind our distribution system, which delivers fresh produce from local and Mainland farmers. For many reasons, small farmers throughout the nation are finding it difficult to sustain their operations, and locally grown produce is becoming increasingly scarce. The once ubiquitous Mānoa lettuce is now a specialty item along with micro-greens such as mesclun and arugula. As much as wholesalers respond to market demand, they also help create it, and we eat what they supply.

While foods imported from the Mainland make up an increasing share of what we eat, Hawai'i is also having an interesting impact on Mainland tastes. The plate lunch — rice, macaroni salad, and a main dish of teriyaki meat or deep-fried seafood, all priced inexpensively — is spreading throughout California and beyond. In addition to independent operators, local plate lunch franchises have burgeoned, particularly on the West Coast, sprouting up as McDonald's had earlier in Hawai'i.

Based in San Francisco, the Hosoda Brothers company is one of the largest dealers of Hawaiian foods, and has branches in Los Angeles and Las Vegas. Owned and operated by Satoru and Carolyn Hosoda, the company was started by Satoru's father and his uncle, who imported Japanese foods, which still comprise the bulk of their business. In the 1950s, the Hosodas distributed their first Hawaiian product, takuan (pickled daikon) made in Waimānalo. Over the years, their Hawaiian list has grown with the Hawaiian diaspora and the spread of the plate lunch, and they now distribute Hawaiian Sun juices, Aloha Shoyu, frozen saimin, kālua pork, Zippy's chili, ox tail soup, several brands of Portuguese sausages, poi, fresh 'ahi, Diamond Bakery crackers, Jade brand cracked seeds, Kaua'i cookies, Lion Coffee, papaya seed dressing, manapua, sea salt, Island Princess chocolates — the list goes on and on. Hosoda Brothers represents over fifty different local producers, and is always looking for other local products to introduce on the Mainland.

The rise in demand for Hawaiian foods comes from local transplants to the Mainland, but Satoru has observed a recent trend in what might be called the Laulau Effect. "Walk into any plate lunch place," he says, "and you will see all kinds of people, not just people from Hawai'i." When he first started supplying laulau, Satoru was certain it would quickly hit a limit and level out on the assumption that the lū'au leaves, pork, and fish combination steamed in ti leaves would appeal only to people from Hawai'i. But to his surprise, the demand grew and continues to grow along with the increasing popularity of plate lunches, and the only conclusion he can draw is that laulau now has a universal appeal. "I am just amazed," he says, "about the amount of laulau we distribute."

Laulau will never become as popular as hamburgers, but it is a rising star in the Mainland fast food scene. The L&L Hawaiian Barbecue website lists its locations in nine Mainland states: California (111), Oregon (2), Washington (4), Texas (1), Utah (2), Nevada (9), Colorado (2), Arizona (2), and New York (1). All of these outlets feature laulau as part of their standard menu. Laulau recipes are available online, some suggesting spinach as a substitute for lū'au leaves, and salted cod for butterfish or salmon. Even the Food Network has a recipe. Laulau has infiltrated the mainstream.

When Iceberg lettuce was first introduced to Hawai'i, no one could have guessed that it would become a local staple. Plate lunches are now exposing Mainlanders to laulau, kālua pork, teriyaki chicken and beef, chicken katsu, the loco moco, saimin, SPAM musubi, and other local delicacies, and all signs point to their increasing popularity. The day may arrive when the plate lunch will have permeated the nation.

The Lettuce and Laulau Effect can happen only with a distribution system operated by people like the Asakuras and the Hosodas, who connect different regions together, allowing local foods to go national, and national foods to go local. Any item can be inserted into the network and sent somewhere else, and while not all of them will make it — Satoru notes that poi has not reached a broad market — the distribution system, working largely out of public sight, remains a powerful arbiter of taste, capable of making people eat Iceberg lettuce on tropical islands or hot laulau in cold places.

George Tanabe retired in 2006 from the University of Hawai'i at Mānoa after teaching in the Religion Department for twenty-nine years. He lives in Waialua, where he grew up on a lotus root farm.

A Duck, Duck Here

June Watanabe

The ducks came later.

Soon after that, duck eggs started showing up.

And all Daniel Yee had wanted to do was to farm the 1.5 acres of Kahaluʻu land he and his wife, Amy, bought thirty-five years ago. But for Yee, a gift of twenty ducks turned out to be serendipitous. The ducks, since multiplied to more than 200, have become part of the farm's cycle of cultivation, and the eggs — fresh or salted by Amy — are prized by those lucky enough to be able to share the Yees' bounty.

Cookbook author June Tong is one. Amy Yee donates eggs whenever Tong needs them for cooking demonstrations and classes she holds, including those for the Miss Narcissus and Miss Chinatown contestants. "There's a shortage of duck eggs right now," Tong said, so the Yee largesse is especially welcome.

Daniel Yee retired as a physics professor at Chaminade University two years ago but still teaches a few classes. "I'm a part-time teacher, a full-time farmer, because ducks have to eat seven days a week," he chuckled.

It's also because the self-described Palōlō-born "city slicker" has discovered he's a farmer at heart, finding an emotional satisfaction in planting the land that perhaps he didn't have in dealing with the science of matter and energy. But always seeking to "recycle everything," Yee's scientific savvy has come in handy as he continues to "nurse the land and bring it to fruition."

Pointing to a huge mound of old cuttings sitting at the entrance to his property, he proclaims, "I feel this is gold! The tree trimmers are so happy to dump it on my property and I use it to nourish the land. To me, it's brown gold. I let it ferment and turn to compost and I put it on my plants."

Likewise, the ducks can't rely on their egg-laying charms to pay the rent. After all, "the plants need fertilizer," he said.

So he keeps shifting their enclosures, depending on which plot needs rejuvenation. The ducks now are housed in the banana groves, but Yee has already cleared away a patch where taro grew and soon the quackers will do their job there, eating weeds, slugs, maggots, and worms, while naturally "preparing" the soil.

"It's good for the ducks and the plants," said Amy, who was an educational assistant at Kaiser High School before retiring. She loves plants, but emphasizes she is "no farmer!"

A walk around their rural spread — a sloping, lushly landscaped piece of property with a natural pond just right for ducks — attests to the success of the symbiotic relationship.

Hawaiian taro — planted initially for a brother who is on the low-fat, Wai'anae diet — defines one pathway that's well-waddled by the ducks. Acerola cherries, pomelo, lychee, guavas, mangos, avocados, star fruit, kumquats, chestnuts, Hawaiian vee border the property. "These are calamansi limes," Yee said, snapping off a few green-yellow fruit. "The Chinese use it for medicine, but they're good in iced tea, too."

Amy Yee stripped some leaves off the "curry tree. You just put the leaves in soup or stew. It doesn't have the coloring, but it tastes like curry," she said. Here and there grow ti plants, red and pink torch ginger, white ginger, birds of paradise.

As the tour continued, a black cat darted by, one of twenty that also call the Yee farm home. The felines don't bother the ducks, but do keep rats and birds away from the duck feeds. For everything there is a reason.

Yee, who went to Saint Louis School, the University of Dayton, and the University of Hawai'i, never envisioned he would one day be toiling — albeit on a much smaller scale — in his uncle's boots. Figuratively, that is. Uncle Tim Yee owned a thousand-duck farm at the spot in which KGMB-TV now sits on Kapi'olani Boulevard.

Still, "I always wanted to be a farmer," Daniel Yee said. That probably was in the back of his mind when he and Amy bought the Kahalu'u property for $18,000 in 1960. Over the years, however, with the Yees living in Hawai'i Kai, the unused property became a dumping ground for abandoned cars.

A couple of years before he retired, "I said I had to reclaim the land. My philosophy is that I am only the steward of this land."

He hauled away about two dozen wrecks and more than sixty loads of trash. Using old fences, recycled wood, he built his own fences and a shed with an overhang to provide shade over a wooden table and four old dining chairs. He carries a cellular phone, but has it turned off most of the time.

When Yee finally retired, he began "to nurse the land and bring it to fruition." He drives forty minutes from his Hawai'i Kai home to the farm every day, usually spending a whole day tending to plants and ducks.

The latter came by accident. Yee had become friends with Gigi Cocquio, a priest who runs the Hoa 'āina o Mākaha Farm in Wai'anae, when both protested the eviction of Hansen's Disease patients from Hale Mohalu years ago. Cocquio had some extra ducks and passed them along to the fledgling farmer. It was Cocquio, Yee said, who "instilled me with environmental consciousness."

Still, in the early days, things weren't exactly ducky. "The problem was that they started laying eggs," he said of the flock.

In time, however, Yee learned how to make them an integral part of the farm. And, lest you forget this is a farm, not a zoo, the ducks don't always hang around 'til retirement. In fact, besides the ducks, the Yees also raise geese, bought as day-old goslings in batches of about three dozen.

"We raise (the geese) to table size, about sixteen pounds," Yee said. Then they, like many of the ducks, end up in Chinese restaurants, on the menu the same day they are purchased because the owners "like them fresh."

Right now, there are four geese keeping company with the ducks, who usually number between 200 and 250, ranging in age from one month to a couple of years. Yee buys the ducks as babies from the Mainland for two dollars each.

Most of the eggs are given away or used in cooking by Amy, but extras are often sold to people who have found out about the ducks through word of mouth. (Amy was adamant I not give away the farm's address, saying she did not want people showing up expecting to buy the eggs, which are never in plentiful supply.)

While "every day is an Easter (duck) egg hunt in the coop," now is the down season for egg laying, she said. Only about sixty eggs are laid daily, compared to upwards of 200 during the spring peak. Depending on the type of duck, individual production varies: Annually, Peking ducks will each lay about 150 eggs; Indian Runners, 200; the golden, 300, Amy said.

With the minimal sales of the ducks, geese, and eggs (and giving away of fruits and vegetables), "we don't make enough money to make it as a business," said Amy.

But Daniel, who admits University of Hawai'i agriculture experts advised him early on that he couldn't really make a living out of farming, isn't dissuaded. The scientist in him "calculated the costs and I feel sure I can support myself."

It's probably a matter of getting his ducks in order.

June Watanabe joined the *Honolulu Star-Bulletin* in 1980 and has been an assistant city editor and reporter, covering government and politics, the University of Hawai'i, and small businesses. She is currently the Kokua Line columnist for the *Honolulu Star-Bulletin*. This article was reprinted with permission from the *Star-Bulletin* and first appeared on November 22, 1995.

Taking Her
to the Open Market

Wing Tek Lum

Scales glisten;
pink whiskers jut out.
Some are the color
of mud, others
recall the embroidery
of coats placed
on babes one month old.
Fat, round, small:
they lay on the crushed
ice, stall after stall.

"Look at the fresh fish!"
I exclaim, eager to impress
on her our respect
for the old
ways, and that I know
how to tell the firmness
a poached flesh will have
by the bulging
of its eyes, the blood
in the gills.

"They are dead,"
she replies. Taken aback,
I see
through her Hong Kong eyes
that fresh
means leaning over
a galvanized pan, eyeing
closely through the running
water at that
cluster of darting
shadows, seeking out the one
swimming most
vigorously: in demonstration
that it
has not yet
passed the point of no return.

"We have,"
I mutter, "killed off
more than germs."

Wing Tek Lum is a Honolulu businessman and poet. "Taking Her to the Open Market" appears in his first collection of poetry, *Expounding the Doubtful Points*, published by Bamboo Ridge Press in 1987.

Ua Kū ka Hale, Ua Pa`a ka Hale

Hawaiian House Blessing

Kalena Silva

Editor's Note: Originally written in Hawaiian as the narration for one of several `Aha Pūnana Leo videotapes on contemporary Hawaiian culture, this article was adapted for publication here in both Hawaiian and English translation.

"Life until one creeps and is weak-eyed with age, until one sprawls like a withered pandanus leaf, until one must be carried about in a hammock, until one reaches the extremity of life!"
— Ancient Hawaiian saying wishing a person long life with years so numerous that he or she enters deep into fragile, old age.

When a baby is born, its *piko*, umbilical cord, is cut, enabling it to enter the world and, if all goes well, to enjoy a long, healthy life. This is the root of the traditional Hawaiian thinking about a house that is blessed — its *piko* is cut, and it emerges into the world as a place which provides many years of shelter for the family that will live in it.

Before the house is blessed, many different things need to be done. As soon as it is known who will conduct the house blessing, family members and

"Ola a kolopūpū, a haumaka'iole, a pala lau hala, a ka'i kōkō, a kau i ka puaaneane!"
— He 'ōlelo kahiko e ho'opuka 'ia no ke ola lō'ihi o ke kanaka e o'o loa ai kona mau makahiki a komo loa aku ho'i i loko o ka wā hapauea.

Ke hānau mai ka pēpē, he 'oki 'ia kona piko e puka mai ai 'o ia i ke ao mālāmalama a, ke maika'i ka noho 'ana, e ola lō'ihi ai nō ho'i 'o ia. 'O kēia ke kumu o ka mana'o no ka hale hou ke ho'ola'a 'ia — he 'oki 'ia kona piko e puka mai ai 'o ia he wahi e malu lō'ihi ai ka 'ohana e noho ana ma loko ona.

Ma mua o ka ho'ola'a 'ana i ka hale, ua nui nā māhele hana like 'ole e maka'ala ai. Aia a maopopo mai ke kanaka nāna ka hale e ho'ola'a, ho'omaka ka 'ohana me nā hoaaloha e ho'omākaukau. He mea nui ke komo o nā hō'ailona no uka a me nā hō'ailona no kai i loko o ka ho'ola'a 'ana.

49

friends begin preparations. Natural symbols from both the land and the ocean are an important part of the blessing.

Family members gather plants that are woven together to make the *piko* which looks like a large open lei with a section hanging down from its center. They look for plants with good associated meanings that will bring blessings and long life to the house and those who live in it.

Pili grass may be woven into the *piko* because *pili* also means to cling to or to remain nearby, keeping family members close to one another. *Kupukupu* fern may be used because *kupu* also means to sprout, enabling love and all good things to grow. Kukui nut kernels, traditionally burned to provide light in darkness, bring insight, knowledge, and wisdom. *Lāʻī*, ti leaf, wards off malevolent forces. *ʻUlu*, breadfruit, sounds like *ulu*, to grow, and enables those living in the house to flourish.

Many other kinds of plants may be woven into the *piko*. Some people use introduced plants like the *manakō*, mango, to cultivate the *mana*, power, to *kō*, fulfill, all of their desires. Some people also use the *puakenikeni*, the "ten cents flower," to attract financial prosperity.

When the *piko* is complete, it is hung above the main doorway of the house. When its middle section is cut, the house is born.

ʻOhiʻohi ka ʻohana i nā meakanu e wili ʻia a paʻa i loko o ka piko he kohu lei hāmama me kahi ʻāpana o waena e lewalewa iho ana i lalo. ʻImi ʻia ka meakanu e launa maikaʻi mai ana ka manaʻo a ola ka hale a me ka poʻe e noho ana ma loko.

ʻO ka lau o ke pili ka mea e pili a launa maikaʻi ai ka poʻe o ka hale. ʻO ke kupukupu ka mea e kupu aʻe ai ke aloha a me nā mea maikaʻi a pau. ʻO ke kukui ka mea e komo ai ka mālamalama, ka ʻike, me ka naʻauao. ʻO ka lāʻī ka mea e pale ai i ka ʻino. ʻO ka ʻulu ka mea e ulu ikaika aʻe ai ko ka hale. Ua nui hou aku nā ʻano meakanu ʻē aʻe e wili ʻia i loko o ka piko. Makemake nō hoʻi kekahi poʻe i nā meakanu malihini ma Hawaiʻi nei e like hoʻi me ka manakō e mana ai ka ʻohana a kō ko lākou mau makemake a pau. Makemake nō hoʻi kekahi poʻe i ka puakenikeni e lako mau ai ka ʻohana i ke kālā.

Ke paʻa ka piko, he hoʻokau ʻia i luna o ka puka komo o ka hale. Ke ʻoki ʻia kona ʻāpana o waena, ua hānau maila kahi hale hou.

Kiʻi pū ka ʻohana i ka iʻa e launa maikaʻi mai ana ka manaʻo a ola ka hale. He weke ʻula ke waiho ʻia ma waho pono o ka puka komo no ka makemake e "wehe" ʻia ka hale a hāmama e komo mai ai hoʻi ka poʻe me nā mea maikaʻi a pau i loko. He ʻamaʻama ke waiho ʻia ma loko pono o ka puka komo no ka makemake e

The family also uses fish with good associated meanings to bless the new house. *Weke 'ula* is placed outside the main doorway because it sounds like *wehe*, to open, bidding visitors and all good things to enter the house. *'Ama'ama* is placed inside because it sounds like *mā'ama'ama*, brightly lit, ensuring light, knowledge and wisdom inside the house.

On the day of the blessing, family members and friends gather in front of the main doorway of the house at noon. Noon is an auspicious time because *"kau ka lā i ka lolo"* (the sun rests on the brain). It is when all things are in clear view and when no shadows are cast to disrupt the proceedings of the blessing.

As soon as the *piko* is hung above the doorway, and the fish are placed inside and out, the *wā kapu,* sacred period, starts. During this period, everyone gathered remains respectfully silent in anticipation of the blessing ritual and the subsequent birth of the house.

The owner of the house thanks all who have gathered, then prays that God's love and blessings be bestowed upon everyone and everything done that day. The person conducting the blessing then begins to chant the house blessing prayer. The prayer begins, *"Ua kū ka hale, ua pa'a ka hale,"* (The house stands, the house is complete) and asks several major Hawaiian deities

"mā'ama'ama" 'o loko, a nui ho'i ka 'ike a me ka na'auao.

Ma ka lā o ka 'aha ho'ola'a, 'ākoakoa mai nā 'ohana me nā hoaaloha ma mua o ka puka komo o ka hale i ke awakea. Maika'i ke awakea no ka mea he "kau ka lā i ka lolo," a ho'i ke aka i loko o ke kino a mōakāka ka nānā 'ana o nā mea a pau — 'a'ohe ili iki iho ho'i o ke aka ma 'ō a ma 'ane'i e hilihewa ai nā hana o ka 'aha ho'ola'a.

Aia a ho'okau 'ia ka piko i luna o ka puka komo a waiho 'ia ho'i ka i'a ma loko me ka i 'a ma waho, ho'omaka ka wā kapu — he wā 'ihi'ihi ia e hāmau ai ka leo o kānaka a e kau ai ho'i kahi mana'o ma luna o ka ho'ola'a a ho'ohānau 'ana i ka hale.

Mahalo ke kanaka nona ka hale i nā 'ohana me nā hoaaloha i 'ākoakoa mai, a pule nō ho'i 'o ia i ke akua nāna e pāhola mai i ke aloha me ka pōmaika'i ma luna o ka po'e a me nā hana a pau o ia lā. A pau ka pule 'ana, ho'omaka ke kanaka nāna ka ho'ola'a 'ana e kau aku i ke mele pule ho'ola'a hale. Ho'omaka ka pule 'ana penei, "Ua kū ka hale, ua pa'a ka hale," me ke noi pū 'ana e kū lō'ihi ka hale me ke kau nui mai o ke ola me nā pōmaika'i ma luna ona.

I ka noa 'ana a'e o ka pule, pau ka wā kapu. Me ka wai pa'akai 'alaea o kāna 'apu e pa'a ana, pīkai hele ke kanaka ho'ola'a hale ma ke kō'ai 'ākau a puni ka hale. Na ia pīkai 'ana e pale aku i nā mea kūpono 'ole me nā mea maika'i 'ole a pau e lapu a kolohe mai ai.

to ensure a long life and many blessings upon the house.

The chanter's final words, "'*Āmama, ua noa*," signal the conclusion of the sacred period. The person blessing the house uses his fingertips to sprinkle water mixed with '*alaea* salt (salt mixed with ocherous earth) from a coconut shell while moving clockwise around the house. The '*alaea* salt water wards off malevolent forces that might cause harm or mischief.

After the water is sprinkled, the time has finally arrived to give birth to the house by cutting its *piko*. The owner of the house assumes this responsibility and, with the help of a family member holding a wooden board in back of the *piko*, cuts it cleanly with an adze, giving life to the new dwelling.

Everyone gathered now celebrates and enjoys each other's company inside the newly born house. Each member of the family living in the house eats at least a small portion of both ritual fishes.

After the celebration, the owner of the house sets aside the portion of the *piko* which has been cut and buries it with the remains of the fishes in the ground near the house. Some people remove the *piko* from above the doorway and bury it, as well. Others, however, prefer to leave the foliage to dry above the doorway as a meaningful reminder of the life and

A pau ka pīkai 'ana, 'o ka manawa nō ia e ho'ohānau mai ai i ka hale ma ke 'oki 'ana i ka piko. Na ke kanaka nona ka hale ia hana a, me ke kōkua o ka 'ohana e pa'a ana i kahi 'āpana papa lā'au ma hope, 'oki 'o ia i ka piko me ke ko'i a moku loa, a hānau mai ho'i kahi hale hou.

'O ka wā nō ho'i kēia e launa ho'ohau'oli ai nā po'e a pau i loko o ia hale i ho'ola'a a ho'ohānau 'ia maila. He 'ai kēlā me kēia kanaka e noho ana ma ka hale he 'āpana li'ili'i o nā i'a 'elua.

Ho'oka'awale ke kanaka nona ka hale i ka 'āpana piko i 'oki 'ia a me ke koena i'a no ke kanu 'ana i ka lepo o ka pā hale ma hope o ka pā'ina. 'O kekahi po'e ho'i, he waiho nō ma ka puka komo i wehi kāhiko e ho'omana'o mau mai ana i ke ola o ka hale.

He mau makahiki pōkole wale iho nei nō i hala, e ho'ola'a 'ia ana nō nā hale ma Hawai'i nei me ke kālele pū nō na'e ma luna o nā loina ho'omana Kalikiano. E moe mālie mai ana ka hana ho'ola'a hale o ka wā kahiko, 'a'ole e mālama nui 'ia ana e ka po'e. Ua ho'āla 'ia kēia hana kahiko no ka 'ike ē he kūhohonu a waiwai loa kona mau 'ao'ao 'o ka 'ike ku'una, ka pili 'uhane, ka 'ōlelo, a me ka lawena.

'Oiai ua nui nā loina Hawai'i kahiko o kēia 'ano ho'ola'a 'ana, ua komo kekahi mau loina o kēia au e like ho'i blessings bestowed upon the house.

Only a few years ago, Hawaiian homes were blessed mainly as prescribed by Christian traditions. The traditional Hawaiian house blessing ritual was not being performed by many people. However, when it became apparent that the ritual contains valuable Hawaiian knowledge, spiritual beliefs, language use, and behaviors, people sought to revive it.

Although the ritual mainly reflects traditional Hawaiian beliefs and practices, some modern practices have been incorporated, like the Christian prayer said by the home owner. Such modern practices enable people to integrate the ancient ritual with their own personal religious beliefs.

Increasingly in Hawaiʻi today, people are using the traditional house blessing not only for houses, but also for other kinds of buildings like offices and schools. And some Hawaiian medium education programs have adapted the ritual by cutting a *piko* at the beginning of each school year to signify the "rebirth" of the programs and to ask for blessings upon them.

With its old and new aspects comfortably integrated, the revitalized house blessing ritual appears to have a healthy future.

me ka pule Kalikiano ma ka hoʻomaka ʻana. Pēlā nō hoʻi e launa maikaʻi ai me nā manaʻo hoʻomana o ka poʻe o kēia manawa.

Ke ʻike ʻia nei nō ka māhuahua ʻana aʻe o ka hoʻolaʻa hale ʻana i waena o ka poʻe ma Hawaiʻi nei, ʻaʻole ʻo ka hale noho wale nō, akā, ʻo ka hale keʻena hana a me ka hale kula pū kekahi. A ua hōʻano hou aku kekahi mau papahana kaiapuni Hawaiʻi ma ka mālama ʻana i ke ʻoki piko ma ka hoʻomaka ʻana o kēlā me kēia makahiki kula i hō ʻailona no ka "hānau" hou ʻana o ia mau papahana a no ke noi ʻana i nā pōmaikaʻi.

ʻOiai ua ʻāwili pū ʻia nā ʻaoʻao kahiko a me nā ʻaoʻao hou o ka hoʻolaʻa hale ʻana i kēia manawa, e māhuahua aʻe ana nō paha i kēia mua aku.

Live Well

mai'a, kalo, 'uala, 'ulu, niu

Hawai'i's
First Celebrity Chef

Bob Dye

Hawai'i's first celebrity chef was a man named Robert von Oehlhoffen, who styled himself a baron, claimed to be from a titled German family, and became King David Kalākaua's master of French cuisine in the late nineteenth century. Some people were skeptical of his boast of being a baron, but everyone who met him agreed that, at the least, he looked like a baron, being a man of "striking appearance, with graceful manners." Those who tasted his food, however, were in no doubt that he was a superb chef. After attending a royal dinner in 1874, a journalist wrote that the feast was "a triumph of taste and art, and reflecting much credit on Mr. R. von Oehlhoffen, His Majesty's Butler." It was, he claimed, "far superior to anything before served in Hawai'i." The menu was printed on white satin.

Who taught von Oehlhoffen how to cook is not known, but the design of his menus and the dishes he prepared suggest he was, to some extent, influenced by the same forces that shaped Auguste Escoffier, "the king of chefs, and the chef of kings." Like Escoffier, von Oehlhoffen was described as "a meticulous person and a strict disciplinarian." In Hawai'i, the court chamberlain reported: "The smallest detail of serving the royal table was of greatest importance to him."

Who was this man? Von Oehlhoffen arrived in Hawai'i, it is thought, during King Lot's reign as Kamehameha V, sometime before 1872, as a cook on a sailing vessel. Befriended by Colonel David Kalākaua, a noted epicurean who served as chamberlain to the king, von Oehlhoffen's timing proved to be as exquisite as his manners. He had arrived at the right place at the right time, and met the best friend a chef could ever have.

Lot was not a social man. He relied on his chamberlain, Kalākaua, to entertain royally. Since most of the distinguished visitors were from Europe, some of them royalty, Kalākaua was in need of a master of French cuisine. Von Oehlhoffen filled the bill with distinction.

Von Oehlhoffen's arrival in Hawai'i came at a time when faraway events made it conceivable these isolated islands would become the crossroads of the Pacific. The opening of the Suez Canal in North Africa and the completion of the Pacific railroad across North America, both in 1869, made it possible to circumnavigate the world without sailing around either Horn — and to do so in style, comfort, and even luxury.

A rumor spread that the British Cunard steamship company or an American competitor would begin a service that would carry passengers from the British colonies of Australia and New Zealand to San Francisco via Honolulu, across the continent by train to New York City and, at last, sail them on to Mother England. But it was an Australian line that opened the route from Sydney to San Francisco, and its ship, *Wonga Wonga*, steamed into Honolulu Harbor on April 19, 1870, on its inaugural voyage.

Politically connected local businessmen immediately saw an opportunity to attract sophisticated world travelers to spend some days in exotic Hawai'i. But, for that to happen, they argued, a first-class hotel with a gourmet dining room within a few blocks of the harbor was necessary. Almost immediately, a public/private partnership was proposed to bring the dream to reality. Lot looked favorably on a proposal from two of his cabinet officers for the government to build such a hotel on their land and lease it to a private operator. Soon, construction was begun and the Hawai'i tourism industry was born.

The building was constructed of concrete blocks made on the site. Work was begun on May 17, 1871; the 120-foot-by-90-foot building was completed by the end of that year. Total cost, including land, building, and furnishings, was $116,528.15. It was leased to Allan Herbert, a businessman. Almost immediately, Herbert hired von Oehlhoffen to be chef de cuisine.

The formal opening of this new extravaganza, named the Hawaiian Hotel, was held on Thursday evening, February 29, 1872, a leap year. Some 250 people attended the spectacular ball and lavish banquet. The grounds were illuminated by torches and Chinese lanterns. Guests entered along a driveway that ended under a canopy of tamarind and algaroba trees. The entrance to the hotel, front and rear, was distinguished by massive stone stairways. Flowering plants were everywhere, and the verandahs, supported by wooden pillars, were festooned with vines of clematis and passion fruit.

For the grand opening, the dining room was transformed into a ballroom where the band of the household troops, under the baton of Frank Medina, played eloquent music until the early hours of the next morning.

Before the dancing began, guests toured the hotel and grounds. The three-story hotel and its lushly landscaped gardens occupied an entire block of downtown Honolulu bounded by Hotel, Richards, Beretania, and Alakea streets. The forty-two guest rooms were lighted by gas lamps and had no running water. There were bathrooms with hot and cold water and water closets on each floor, as well as plunge baths in the yard. An observation cupola topped the slate-roof structure and a large billiard room, with three fine tables made of choice California laurel oak, was situated in the basement. A bar and card table were at its east end. Room rates were three dollars a night, or fifteen dollars for a week.

The Hawaiian Hotel's important neighbor was `Iolani Palace, a small building that served as the official residence of the king, but was ill-suited as an indoor venue for social events. Because of the new hotel's proximity, spacious grandeur and fine dining room, the king's chamberlain used it to entertain guests in the royal manner. In turn, the hotel was a preferred venue for persons who wished to entertain the king. When Kalākaua took a suite in the hotel, this adjunct of the palace came to be called the Royal Hawaiian Hotel.

As its promoters had promised, famous world travelers did indeed take up residence at the Hawaiian Hotel, using it as a base to explore the island chain. Early reports were glowing. The Hawaiian "is a surprisingly excellent hotel," wrote Charles Nordhoff, America's most respected journalist. "This is the perfection of a hotel," noted Isabella Lucy Bird, the most famous lady traveler of her day. In a testimony to von Oehlhoffen's influence, she added, "The great dining room is delicious. It has no curtains, and its decorations are cool and pale. Its windows look upon tropical trees in one direction and up to cool mountains in the other. Piles of bananas, guavas, limes, and oranges decorate the tables at each meal, and strange vegetables, fish, and fruits vary the otherwise stereotyped American hotel fare."

Von Oehlhoffen's kitchen was in the basement. Its modern French cooking range was capable of "rapidly cooking meals for 500 people." A dumbwaiter connected the kitchen to the dining room, which accommodated 180 guests. Diners were naval officers, families of wealthy planters in Honolulu for the season, health-seekers from California, resident boarders, whaling captains, tourists from the British Pacific colonies, and townspeople.

Ms. Bird noted there were no female domestics. "The host is a German, the manager an American, the steward a Hawaiian, and the servants are all Chinamen, in spotless white linen, with pigtails coiled round their heads, and an air of superabundant good nature."

Honolulu families were enticed to the hotel by an ice cream parlor that was open every evening from six to nine. Also popular were the hot- and cold-water baths, which were open from sunrise until midnight. The price of a single bath was fifty cents. Comfort and privacy were promised, with female attendants available to assist women and children.

When Kalākaua was elected king in 1874, he asked von Oehlhoffen to instruct his envoy, Col. Curtis Pi'ehu I'aukea, in European etiquette: "Each gesture had to be learned with just the right degree of deference." Years later, when I'aukea represented Hawai'i at the coronation of Tsar Alexander III and Tsarina Marie Fedorovna in Moscow, he thanked "the fates" for von Oehlhoffen's instruction on diplomatic procedure, which stood him "in very good stead," he reported.

To ensure that von Oehlhoffen had the freshest food, proprietor Herbert contracted with local fishermen and farmers, paying one gardener more than a thousand dollars a year. He established a "ranch" in Kalihi where producers could bring chickens, ducks, turkeys, geese, and pigs to be fattened for the kitchen. So successful were his efforts that von Oehlhoffen had fresh eggs and butter, milk and cream for his sauces, and a wide variety of other fresh food stuffs for his menu. They were, according to the Hawaiian Guide Book:

- Meats: Beef, mutton, pork, and all kinds of poultry.

- Vegetables: Irish and sweet potatoes, beans, tomatoes, corn, beets, cabbage, carrots, radishes, onions, turnips, squash, eggplant, cucumbers, taro, breadfruit, yams, and others.

- Fruit: Strawberries, grapes, guavas, oranges, pineapples, bananas, mangoes, pohas, papayas, melons, and more.

For a dinner honoring Kalākaua at the Hawaiian Hotel, von Oehlhoffen prepared for the first course a Windsor soup (calf's feet and chin of veal boiled and thickened with rice flour) with a julienne garnish. The fish course featured Uhu a la Cardinale and mullet with a hollandaise sauce, accompanied by a boiled potato. Anchovies were then served as an hors d'oeuvre.

Preceded by plovers on toast, a roast of spring lamb with mint sauce was next, accompanied by potatoes a la Figaro and a salmy (salmigondis) of wild ducks. The entrees were Epigram of Chicken (presumably breaded and lightly fried in butter) served with stewed tomatoes and followed by Calf's Brain a la Viroli. Next came a serving of asparagus followed by a salad of Chicken Mayonnaise (probably decorated with capers, small-pitted olives, anchovy fillets and quartered hard-boiled eggs), plain lettuce, and cheese.

For dessert, von Oehlhoffen served Cabinet Pudding (egg custard poured over alternate layers of Lady's Fingers soaked in rum or a liqueur, and raisins and crystallized fruit, soaked in rum and baked in an oven for forty-five minutes), confectionery and fruits. The dinner concluded with the serving of Caffe Puss (pousse café), carefully poured layers of ice cold, colorful liqueurs, the order determined by the weight of the liqueur, the heaviest (most sugar) at the bottom and working up to the lightest (most alcohol), topped with heavy cream.

Bon appetit.

In the summer of 1880, von Oehlhoffen was described as "formerly a well-known caterer and master of cuisine in Honolulu," when he opened a hotel at Hālawa, North Kohala, on the Big Island. Called the Kohala Hotel, the wooden structure was located on the main road, opposite the post office. "Aside from the fact that such an establishment must prove a great convenience and comfort to strangers and travelers," wrote a reporter in the *Pacific Commercial Advertiser,* "Robert's well-known taste and skill in the culinary art will prove a great recommendation."

With the Kohala Hotel up and running, Kalākaua asked von Oehlhoffen to accompany him in early 1881 as his personal attendant and keeper of the royal feather cape on a circumnavigation of the world. The choice was controversial. Two "missionary boys," Charles Judd and William Armstrong, who would serve as the king's official aides, made a "mild protest" of the choice. Kalākaua was not deterred. Von Oehlhoffen's impeccable court manners and mastery of European languages would be invaluable. Even Armstrong recognized him as "an educated man of prepossessing appearance and a remarkable linguist," but, he cautioned, also "of intemperate habits" and "unreliability." Throughout the journey, Armstrong complained about von Oehlhoffen and tried to get him fired for misuse of the royal feather cape. But Kalākaua was amused by von Oehlhoffen's antics and would not hear of sending him home.

In May 1883, von Oehlhoffen and a partner opened a restaurant, called the Delmonico, on King Street in Honolulu. The business did not succeed and in October the partners filed for bankruptcy. The following year, von Oehlhoffen and his wife sailed to San Francisco on the *S.S. Alameda*. Their only child, a son named Kalani, stayed behind, according to family tradition, with his Hawaiian mother's relatives. Von Oehlhoffen never returned to Hawai'i. He died on November 10, 1885, in Sacramento, California.

Today, one of von Oehlhoffen's best-known descendants is a giant of a man from Moloka'i named Kimo von Oelhoffen (who has dropped the first "h" in the original name), a veteran 6-foot-4-inch, 299-pound NFL defensive tackle for the Pittsburgh Steelers. Other descendants live in the islands.

Bob Dye is the author of *Merchant Prince of the Sandalwood Mountains: Afong and the Chinese in Hawai'i*, and the editor of the *Hawai'i Chronicles* series of books. His articles on Hawai'i have appeared in *Newsday, The Honolulu Advertiser*, the *Hawaiian Journal of History, Honolulu* magazine, and other journals. "Hawai'i's First Celebrity Chef" appeared in *Spirit of Aloha* magazine in September/October 2005.

By the Book:
Cookbooks in Hawai'i

Willa Tanabe

Cookbooks tell us who we are, who we were, and sometimes who we want to be. In eighteenth century America, cookbooks were at first merely reprints of English works. They were intended for wealthy women to use to direct their often illiterate cooks and servants. However in 1796, an American, Amelia Simmons, self-published *American Cookery, or The Art of Dressing Viands, Fish, Poultry and Vegetables, and the Best Modes of Making Pastes, Puffs, Pies, Tarts, Puddings, Custards and Preserves and All Kinds of Cakes....Adapted to This Country and All Grades of Life.* This cookbook was unique because Simmons included American ingredients — such as corn meal, cranberries, and turkey — not found in England or Europe. She advised using corncobs to smoke bacon, and gave the recipes for Indian slapjacks and Johnny cakes. In short, Simmons adapted her recipes to her specific locale. Taste and place were inextricably linked and this made her book a culinary revolution, a cookbook by an American for Americans.

Hawai'i, too, has a tradition of cookbooks that reflect the history and diverse cooking traditions of the islands. One of the earliest is the *Hawaiian Cook Book*, compiled by the Ladies' Society of Central Union Church. First published in 1882, it was reprinted many times and established a type of cookbook that is still popular today. It was a community-based cookbook compiled from recipes of its membership and sold to raise funds for charitable projects. Today we have compilations of recipes not just from church groups, but schools, businesses, ethnic associations, and service organizations.

Not surprisingly the recipes of the Ladies' Society of Central Union Church reflect the nature of its membership. Divided into the common categories we still use, such as soup, fish, meat, desserts, and so forth, the dishes are overwhelmingly European, similar to those dishes found in the continental United States. A few included local ingredients such as green mangoes boiled with potatoes or lūʻau leaves which, it was noted, one could get from Chinese vegetable vendors. In over 137 pages only two were devoted to Native Hawaiian recipes. They included directions for the preparation of pig in an imu, meats in banana leaves, and puddings such as haupia and kūlolo. Hawaiian foods were treated as special, not everyday fare. The foods of Asian immigrants were not mentioned, although many of the servants who prepared the Western recipes must have been from these immigrant communities.

The most interesting aspect of the *Hawaiian Cook Book* is the names of the contributors, many from the families most intimately connected with the history of Hawaiʻi. We learn that Mrs. C.H. Judd enjoyed sheep's tongue in tomato sauce, Mrs. Charles Dillingham loved ham toast, and Mrs. McCully served black bean soup. A few men even contributed recipes, including many from August Jean Baptiste Marques, a Frenchman who arrived in Hawaiʻi in 1878 and was instrumental in bringing Portuguese to Honolulu as well as serving as King Kalākaua's envoy to Russia.

The Hawaiian Cook Book also included advertisements by community businesses. In the 1909 edition, the Bank of Hawaiʻi promoted paying of bills by cheques. McInerny Shoe Store claimed that "to be satisfied with your shoes makes all other walks of life easier." Bishop Trust Co. announced a new department especially designed to meet the requirements of women and supervised by a woman, Miss J.T. MacIntryre, who had managed a Bishop's Savings Bank for eight years. Clearly cookbooks give us the flavor of a particular time period.

The emphasis on Western recipes with token inclusion of Hawaiian food continued in almost all pre-World War II cookbooks, including those by single authors. *The Helen Alexander Hawaiian Cook Book* (1938) and *Hart's Hawaiian Homes Cook Book* (1930) both contained brief sections on Hawaiian food that included many favorites such as lomi salmon, chicken with lūʻau leaves and coconut, jerked beef, squid and coconut, and many limu dishes. But they rarely mentioned other ethnic dishes, although Hart did note a few simple Chinese and Japanese dishes such as hamburger and Tow Foo (tofu). Often when cookbooks of this period feature an Asian or local recipe, the dish is unrecognizable. *The Epicure in Hawaiʻi* (1938) included a Sai Men recipe that was frequently repeated in later cookbooks. This Sai Men dish topped cooked macaroni with chopped and steamed green onions, mushrooms, mushroom juice, soy sauce, fried bacon, and tuna. This recipe, (more appropriately renamed Saimin-roni) turned up in a 1956 Coral Tuna cookbook.

The economic, political, and social power of ethnic groups rose in post-war Hawai'i and cookbooks became more inclusive. The melting pot ideal was echoed and it was common to find a "Kahuku Spaghetti" recipe, next to "Chinese Pot Roast," next to "SPAM Tempura." The series of cookbooks compiled by the Maui Extension Homemakers Council was a classic of this type. While we distinguished the books by the color of the cover (my family's favorite was the "red" Maui cookbook), the actual titles told of their ongoing popularity: *Our Favorite Recipes* (1959), *More of Our Favorite Recipes* (1964), *Still More of Our Favorite Recipes* (1967), and *Still Many More of Our Favorite Recipes* (1972).

Reading the community cookbooks chronologically reveals changes in family life. Recipes at first were often intended for large, frugal families. They began with a "5 lb. box of chicken thighs," included malassadas that required three pounds of flour and eight to twelve eggs, and expected you to grate your own coconut. The later development of increased travel, eating out, and two-income households with fewer children resulted both in simplified and smaller portioned recipes on the one hand, and sophisticated "new" tastes for dishes such as veal picatta and many varieties of pesto and pasta.

By the 1970s there were so many community-based cookbooks that they began to distinguish themselves by including brief vignettes of the organizing group. Mō'ili'ili Community Center's cookbook, *The Tastes and Tales of Mō' ili'ili* (1997), for example, relates legends and little known facts about the neighborhood. *What's Cooking at Waialua* (1973), compiled by the Waialua Sugar Co. for its seventy-fifty anniversary, asserted that multi-racial cooking was the norm and summarized the culinary contributions of their immigrant community, noting that the Chinese introduced bamboo shoots, water chestnuts, stir-fry, and lotus root (paddys of which still exist in Waialua). The Japanese introduced the marinade now known as teriyaki, along with sushi and sashimi. The Portuguese contributed sweet bread, malassadas, and bean soup, while the Koreans favored chili peppers and kim chee. The Filipinos introduced new vegetables such as long beans, Ilocano spinach, and marungay. The text even mentioned Germans, Scandinavians, and Russians, though no particular recipes from these groups were included. On the whole, community cookbooks reflect our appreciation of ethnic cuisine and cultures and celebrate an everyday approach to food. They are cookbooks written by insiders for insiders.

While community cookbooks often take our understanding of the customs, ingredients or even history of certain cuisines for granted, expository cookbooks interpret and explain cuisines. Their texts are half essay, half recipes, transmitting the context of foods, not mere directions. One of the earliest and most influential works in this vein was *Hawaiian and Pacific Foods: A Cook Book of Culinary Customs and Recipes Adapted for the American Hostess (1940)* by Katherine Bazore. Bazore was a home economist at the University of Hawai'i from 1939 to 1961. As a Mid-Westerner, she was unfamiliar with but entranced by the exotic ingredients and varied cuisines of her students. She began her book with a sketch of Hawaiian history and gave a pronunciation guide for the seven separate cuisines that she discussed: Hawaiian, Samoan, Chinese, Japanese, Korean, Filipino, and Portuguese. Before she presented any recipes, she described typical ingredients, serving customs, menus, and possible substitutions for unavailable ingredients. Her work displayed careful research. She noted, for example, some differences among Filipino dishes of Ilocano, Tagalog, and Visayan background. This book was not merely useful and informative, it also put the stamp of approval of the academic world on ethnic foods. It underscored the idea that "ethnic" food was worthy of inclusion and made it easier to be proud of one's cultural heritage.

Cookbooks centered on the cuisine of a single ethnic group flourished in the late twentieth century. Often produced in celebration of the anniversaries of first migrations to Hawai'i or the renaissance of Hawaiian cultural practices, *Hawai'i Filipina's Favorite Recipes* (1974) by the Filipino Women's League, *Okinawan Cookery and Culture* (1975), compiled by the United Okinawan Association, *Portuguese Cuisine in Hawai'i* (1982) by John Peru, *Recipes from the Heart of Hawai'i's Puerto Ricans* (1999), compiled for the United Puerto Rican Association of Hawai'i, and *Cooking in Old Hawai'i* by Tamar Luke Pane'e (2 vols., 1987-90) all reflect native and ethnic pride.

Expository cookbooks continued to be produced, each offering differing insights to Hawai'i's food. Rachel Laudan, another University of Hawai'i professor, from England, wrote *The Food of Paradise: Exploring Hawai'i's Culinary Heritage* (1996). Her index of recipes by ethnicity attests to the changing pattern of our population. Like Bazore, some 55 years earlier, she includes recipes that are Chinese, Filipino, Portuguese, Korean, Hawaiian, and Japanese, but she also adds categories of kama'āina, Okinawan, Southeast Asian, and local foods, while omitting Samoan food. Her recipes follow a series of insightful essays with delightful titles such as "Pidgin, Pork and the Portuguese," and "Malasadas and Andagi: Doughnuts from Two Ends of the Earth."

It is not only outsiders who write expository cookbooks. *The Island Plate: 150 Years of Recipes and Food Lore from The Honolulu Advertiser* (2006) by Wanda Adams, born and raised on Maui, is a wonderful history of food as chronicled in the local newspaper. She discusses how women learned to cook, the impact of rationing in World War II, tiki kitsh cooking, plate lunch and local foods, the critical importance of the home economists at the Hawaiian Electric and gas companies, the rise of regional and fusion cuisine, and the influence of the food editors of the local newspapers. In her last chapter, she ponders the impact of our concerns with health and weight loss along with the popularity of the Food Network television programs. Expository cookbooks remind us that food reflects cultural change and recipes are collectible artifacts.

The United States has had different social ideals at different times. Early on, people sought to equal their European ancestors. Later, they praised the integration of our diverse ethnic backgrounds into a melting pot. More recently we celebrated our distinct ethnic backgrounds, seeing our society as a tossed salad of unique ingredients. These ideals are reflected in the cookbooks of Hawai'i. From European to single ethnic and multi-ethnic dishes, the cookbooks we use reflect our notions of ourselves and our place and chart the history of our identities.

Willa Tanabe is a retired professor of Japanese Art History and former dean of the School of Hawaiian, Asian and Pacific Studies at the University of Hawai'i. She continues to write and speak on art and culture in Japan and Hawai'i.

the last mango
of summer
CANE HAUL ROAD, LTD., HAWAII

Mango: Jelly Substitute

Yu no mi,
Ai kelek maenggo.
Ai yuzu kuk da maenggo.
Ai kuk li bit shuga,
Braun shuga ya kukom.
An den putom aw lin a bato.
An den bambai wen ai go jringk kawfi
Ai teik da bred,
I meik da maenggo awn tawp
Wit maenggo aez mai jele, ai itom.

You know me, I collect mango. I used to cook the mango. I cook the mango. I put little bit sugar, brown sugar, yeah, cook 'em. And then put 'em all in a bottle. And then bumbai {later} when I go drink coffee, I take the bread, I make the mango on top. With mango as my jelly, I eat 'em.

*This is an excerpt from **Ernest Richardson***'s interview in Lanai`i Ranch: The People of Kō`ele and Keōmuku *(Center for Oral History, 1989). It has been transcribed to Carol Odo's Hawai`i Creole English orthography (transcription provided by Charlene Sato) and in English orthography for comparison.*

Easter:
Wahiawā, 1959

Cathy Song

1
The rain stopped for one afternoon.
Father brought out
his movie camera and for a few hours
we were all together
under a thin film
that separated the rain showers
from that part of the earth
like a hammock
held loosely by clothespins.

Grandmother took the opportunity
to hang the laundry
and Mother and my aunts
filed out of the house
in pedal pushers and poodle cuts,
carrying the blue washed eggs.

Grandfather kept the children
penned in on the porch,
clucking at us in his broken English
whenever we tried to peek
around him. There were bread crumbs
stuck to his blue gray whiskers.

I looked from him to the sky,
a membrane of egg whites
straining under the weight
of the storm that threatened
to break.

We burst loose from Grandfather
when the mothers returned
from planting the eggs
around the soggy yard.
He followed us,
walking with stiff but sturdy legs.
We dashed and disappeared
into bushes,
searching for the treasures;
the hard-boiled which Grandmother had been simmering
in vinegar and blue color all morning.

2
When Grandfather was a young boy
in Korea,
it was a long walk
to the riverbank,
where, if he were lucky,
a quail egg or two
would gleam from the mud
like gigantic pearls.
He could never eat enough
of them.

It was another long walk
through the sugarcane fields
of Hawai'i,
where he worked for eighteen years,
cutting the sweet stalks
with a machete. His right arm
grew disproportionately large
to the rest of his body.
He could hold three grandchildren
in that arm.

I want to think
that each stalk that fell
brought him closer
to a clearing,
to that palpable field
where from the porch
to the gardenia hedge
that day he was enclosed
by his grandchildren
scrambling around him,
for whom he could at last buy
cratefuls of oranges,
basketfuls of sky blue eggs.

I found three that afternoon.
By evening, it was raining hard.
Grandfather and I skipped supper.
Instead, we sat on the porch
and I ate what he peeled
and cleaned for me.
The scattering of the delicate
marine-colored shells across his lap
was something like what the ocean gives
the beach after a rain.

Cathy Song was the 1982 winner of the Yale Series of Younger Poets competition. She also received the Cades Award for Literature in 1993 and the Shelley Memorial Award from the Poetry Society of America in 1994. "Easter: Wahiawā, 1959" is reprinted from *Picture Bride*, published by Yale University Press in 1983.

OXTAIL SOUP

The Columbia Inn Story: 'We Are Still Family'

Eugene Kaneshiro

The restaurant, the original Columbia Inn, opened in December 1941. This was the old Columbia Inn located at 116 Beretania Street at the corner of Kamanuwai Lane, better known as the "Tin Can Alley," where the burlesque theatre was. I should say that the Columbia Inn at Beretania was known as the "Gem in the Slums" because it was located in the middle, crossroads between Chinatown and all the rooming houses in that whole area.

The people who used to live in that area, the neighborhood, were predominantly single Filipino men who worked at the cannery or as stevedores. Also a lot of Hawaiian, part-Hawaiian families that lived in that River Street, Kukui Street, Nuʻuanu Avenue, Beretania Street, King Street, ʻAʻala Park, that whole area there.

After the war Columbia Inn ran twenty-four hours and got a bar open in 1950. The margin on serving a drink is much more than the profit margin on food. I think the major thing that happened in that bar is my father renovated that area where he put the bar in, besides tables and booths, put this round table in that's kind of high. It had six stools, but usually you had maybe eight people squeezed around the darn thing and for some reason that round table brought the best of conversation out and sometimes could be very mundane conversation, but nevertheless, it was entertaining to people.

The menu

If you look at the menu of the Columbia Inn, it looks generic like the menus from other restaurants that were owned and operated by Okinawans. Predominantly so-called American foods, full complete meals, soup to nuts. Beef liver, veal cutlets, hamburger steak, spaghetti, very standard things. The closest thing to Okinawan food was pig's feet soup, but the popularity of pig's feet soup in the restaurant didn't come about until later.

The sizzling platter was around. I remember having seen a real big sign outside, backlit with fluorescent lights, and it says "Sizzling Rib Steak." I can remember that sizzling platter coming out of the kitchen on the tray that the waitress was carrying and the thing is just a huge plume of smoke trailing. Then, everybody turning around, looking and seeing who's ordering this sizzling rib steak. It was a show in itself.

Family operation

My mom worked in that restaurant. She was a waitress, and practically did everything in that restaurant, except cook. In fact, she worked at Frankie's Café along with her sisters. I'm not really sure how exactly my father met up with her, but it had to be there. Having worked there, then they were working at Columbia Inn together, planning to open that restaurant. In fact, one story is that they were in the restaurant cleaning up the place on the day that the bombs were dropping at Pearl Harbor.

My uncle who was my mother's brother was the cook there, Jason Maeshiro. My uncle George Uehara, who was married to my mother's youngest sister, pulled a stint over there also at the Columbia Inn-Beretania. But, eventually, he became the chef at the new location at Kapiʻolani, the Columbia Inn, Top of the Boulevard. His wife, Betty, was our office manager and helped us with most of the office administrative things — type menus, and all those kinds of things. Eventually her daughter got involved in the restaurant business too, Judy Uehara Koza.

Of course, my cousin Frenchy was there from the beginning to the end. His brother, Robert, joined us after college, but didn't stay too long, but he was instrumental in becoming part of the business when Columbia Inn moved to the Kapiʻolani location. It's really, truly a family business. My understanding is any family member who did work gave a hundred and ten percent and probably more than the regular employees that worked there.

The partnership between my father's older brother Gentaro and my father, Toshi, survived because one, Gentaro, despite being an alien was not interned; and two, my father's draft was deferred until after the war. They were able to operate the Columbia Inn during the war.

The roles kind of like changed, in the later years, before moving the restaurant from downtown to Kapiʻolani. My father eventually moved to the front of the house, leaving the kitchen chores to people that they hired. And then, Gentaro took more like a semi-silent-partner arrangement and allowed my father the leeway to manage the restaurant.

Public relations

In trying to promote the restaurant, my father recognized early on that you cannot just be a restaurant that serves good food at a reasonable price, but you had to draw people in. I can recall he used to go down to United Press International and he used to actually get wire service stories and pictures to put up in the front of the restaurant in the window. People used to stop and look.

And then inside the restaurant, every occasion, he used to dress the restaurant up. If it was Easter, he had Easter eggs and bunnies and stuff like that, and the people used to come in there. Imagine when he's hanging what looked like autumn leaves; imagine Christmas decorations in a restaurant, that's typical. But, Fourth of July, he got flags and bunting. When you had the Cherry Blossom Festival, he had cherry blossoms all over the place.

My father became, in the early 1950s, a Dodgers fan because everybody was rooting for the Yankees, so he took the underdog. But he promoted the heck out of this "Go Dodgers, go." Baseball season, he'd be walking around with a baseball hat, LA, Los Angeles Dodgers. He carried that promotion over to the Kapi'olani restaurant with him. The "Go Dodgers, go" sign was still there, hanging every season.

And you know Chinese New Year? He invited all of the Chinese clubs with their dragons to end up a certain time in front of the Columbia Inn. Gave three, four cases of beer to the firemen and they brought their hook-and-ladder truck in the front there. He bought the fireworks and they joined two fifty-foot strings. And here's this hook-and-ladder truck with this hundred-foot-long firecracker dangling. My father in his Chinese skullcap, and they were taking pictures of him lighting the thing up.

It was truly a gathering place for everyone, including all the gamblers and the crooks. Oh, the cops used to take their shirt off because they didn't want to portray that they were cops, they're a customer. Crooks on the other side of the restaurant. Neutral turf, they got to eat somewheres. It truly was like that, they never bothered each other inside the restaurant.

Restaurant kids

I guess, typical of a lot of restaurant families, the kids were exposed to the restaurant, the kitchen. I can remember going downstairs into the dark storeroom and seeing all the food stacked up over there.

And watching the workers in the kitchen, like our then-chef, Shima-Seikichi Shimabukuro, we used to call him "Uncle Shima" — watching him dress a whole side of beef, taking out all the different parts for the steak and for the stew meat, and all the other parts to grind up to make hamburger and things like that. We used to watch the fry cooks fry up eggs and hamburger steak and everything else. Watching the dishwasher and not realizing that was hard work, but just knowing that there's somebody washing dishes.

I can recall my father teaching me how to give change. Gosh, I wish he was here to confirm this, but I thought that he had a chair that I could stand on, so I can operate the cash register and actually collect and give change properly. Today, you got cash registers that tell you exactly how much change to give, but during those days, it was a mechanical machine and you had to know how to give change.

I know my number-two brother, Dennis, who's couple years younger than I am, I remember him pitching in as a dishwasher at the old Columbia Inn. My brother Norman was too young to help at the old Columbia Inn, but he started with me some years later at the new location of Columbia Inn-Kapi'olani.

Columbia Inn-Kapi'olani

By the time I got into high school, many people began to move out from that area because that Model Cities Program was used to redevelop that whole area. Eventually, because the building we were in was torn down, we were ready to move to a new location.

So, from a small restaurant at Columbia Inn-Beretania Street where he did have a chef there, Shima, who was actually the man cooking all the food, a bigger restaurant required someone with different skills. So, Shima became our number-two man, who we call a sous chef, and George Uehara became the executive chef, and he planned all of the menus, and provided everyone with the recipes, and trained people. So, my father, with that confidence in George, they opened Columbia Inn-Kapi'olani in December 1964.

In the restaurant business, you go from meal period to meal period, it's breakfast, lunch, dinner, and then we were open twenty-four hours, so you got a late-night rush going on after the bars close during those days. You wanted to be there when it was busy because you had to be there. But you also wanted to be there when it's slow because that's when you want to see how you can improve the business to make it better, or that's when usually the problems come up, when it's slow. And so, you end up being there more hours than you really thought you would be. So typically, a twelve-hour, or sixteen-hour, or eighteen-hour day was like average sometimes.

Next generation

One day my father sat me down and said, "I'm going to put the business in your hands." He said, "Big Uncle" — that's Gentaro — "allowed me to run the business. Now I'm going to turn it over to you. I'm going to ask Frenchy to help us, and I'm going to ask your brother Norman to stay on, too. I'm going let you make the decisions from now and you do it your way and I'll just watch you from the sidelines."

He stepped aside from the day-to-day operation of the restaurant and essentially became like the ambassador, like the man who shakes everybody's hands and says hello. He turned the thing over to Frenchy and me when he was not even mid-fifties, early fifties. He died a month short of sixty. Maybe that led to his demise, we don't know. We were essentially operating the business for him, and of course, he was there every single day.

But still, the operation side of things was myself and my cousin Frenchy. My cousin Frenchy worked hard, too. He pulled the hardest shift. He knew that I was raising a family. I had a daughter, an only child. But, even at that, I was so married to the business that I look back and I tell myself, "Wow, man, I missed the best part of my daughter's growing-up years." I used to take her to school and after that never saw her. I used to see her sleeping when I came home at night, but that was the life of the restaurant business.

The name lives on

I guess the experience here is that those Okinawan families, first- and second- and third-generation families and now even the fourth-generation, they all went through this. A lot of them saw their parents working so hard or they had experienced washing dishes, cleaning tables, scrubbing the kitchen, washing the toilets, and all those kinds of things, I think that's what drove them to go out of the restaurant business and make something out of their lives in another field.

Maybe us Kaneshiros, we were maybe too generous. We give away more stuff than we kept, but I think we lived a comfortable life and we were happy with what we were doing. You hear stories about families breaking up because of finances and all those kind of things. I think we were blessed with my father and his older brother, who were able to make sure that we respect each other even though we were co-workers and saw each other on a daily basis, and we are still family.

Eugene Kaneshiro, eldest of three sons born to Fred Toshio and Beatrice Kaneshiro, spent part of his childhood in and around the family-run Columbia Inn in Chinatown. In the mid-1960s, he joined Columbia Inn's management at Kapi'olani Boulevard. Following his father's death in 1981, he and other family members continued to operate their restaurants in Honolulu and Waimalu until the businesses were sold in the mid-1980s. This is an edited excerpt from Eugene's oral history recorded by the Center for Oral History at the University of Hawai'i at Mānoa. He was interviewed by Michi Kodama-Nishimoto, with the transcript originally edited by Cynthia A. Oshiro.

Pupus of the Gods: On Hawaiian Cuisine in America During the Cold War

Lee Siegel

I had my first taste of Hawaiian food in the early 1950s, or at least what was known and celebrated at that time as Hawaiian cuisine just about everywhere in America except perhaps in the Territory of Hawai'i. I can still remember the feel on my fingertips of the crispy coconut-battered jumbo shrimp as I dipped it in the sweet Hawaiian mango ketchup glistening in a little porcelain scallop shell. I remember the delicate crunch between my teeth and then the delectable flavor of the succulent flesh on my tongue. That Kon Tiki Coconut Shrimp at Don the Beachcomber's South Seas Bar and Restaurant on McCadden Place in Hollywood was the best thing I had ever eaten in my entire life, all seven or eight years of it.

Dinner at the Beachcomber's was always sure to inspire transport, enchantment, and reverie. It was a world in which everything was sweet.

"Aloha," the Chinese maitre d' standing by the carved Tiki idol in the entry would say with a slight bow and demure smile. And I'd repeat it back to him — "Aloha"— as if it were the secret password admitting me into paradise.

Lusciously exotic aromas from the kitchen, tinged with coconut and pineapple and accented with Polynesian perfumes of pikake and plumeria, laced the atmosphere of the Hawaiian haven aglow with an eternally crepuscular light from the bloated bellies of blowfish, hurricane lamps, and amber, marine blue, and green glass globes floating with driftwood in the fishing nets draped overhead. The woven frond and tapa-covered walls were adorned with swordfish, gaping shark jaws, bamboo-framed travel posters, lithographs of old Hawai'i, and, most marvelous of all, paintings on lush black velvet of voluptuous grass-skirted, bare-breasted wahines. One danced the hula, another leaned languorously against the sloping trunk of a coco palm, and my favorite girl bathed in a moonlit grotto fed by a shimmering waterfall.

No matter the weather in Hollywood, it was, by the grace of an automatic sprinkler system, sure to drizzle every fifteen minutes outside the windows of Don the Beachcomber's Hawai'i. Fern, bamboo, ti, and birds of paradise were swathed in a tropical mist, and fantastically colored, striped, and dotted reef fish darted and swirled about iridescent coral, shiny shells, and undulant anemones in luminous aquaria. The whispering of waves, melodious strum of ukuleles, and cheerful chatter of eating and drinking connoisseurs of Hawaiian cuisine and culture were a South Pacific soundtrack. At a time when it seemed that the Cold War was precariously on the brink of becoming a nuclear one, Don the Beachcomber's Polynesia was a place of refuge from a harsher real world.

Comfortably enthroned in an expansively fan-backed rattan and wicker chair at our smoothly polished koa table, my mother sipped a gardenia-garnished Puka Puka Punch as my father, the smoke from his cigarette curlicuing out of an abalone shell ashtray, happily quaffed a Zombie from a ceramic Tiki goblet. My younger brother Robert and I were offered two-foot-long straws, one for each of us, so that we could share a giant clam shell full of Keiki Pi-Yi, a non-alcoholic version of a libation normally concocted with light and dark rum, brandy, Curacao, passion fruit liquor, pineapple juice, guava nectar, grenadine, orgeat syrup, and a "secret ingredient." Secret ingredients always seemed to make things taste better.

Because Robert and I competed for the nectarously sugary Pi-Yi, the clam shell bowl would quickly run dry. Then we'd each order our own Menehune Hune served in a hollowed-out pineapple, garnished with an orchid, pineapple slice, maraschino cherry, strip of sugar cane, plastic Tiki stirrer, and a little paper umbrella. It tasted as amazing as it looked, and I was allowed to take the pineapple container, stirrer, and umbrella home. I wished my beverage could have been served flaming like a Pele's Passion, Lava Flow, or Kilauea Killer, but setting a drink on fire required 151-proof rum. The maitre d' did, however, bring me extra maraschino cherries and pineapple slices as consolation. The next morning I'd fill the souvenir of dinner in paradise with Hawaiian Punch for breakfast.

The food at Don the Beachcomber's was as enchanting as the grand grog and dazzling décor: the Polynesian Pupu Platter, lavishly festooned with vanda blossoms, pineapple slices, and coconut shavings, was a fabulous assortment of those delectable coconut-battered deep-fried Kon Tiki shrimp, crispy egg rolls, scrumptious won ton, and chunky pineapple chicken on bamboo skewers.

Much to my embarrassment, my father would perfunctorily ask the waiter about the ingredients in the egg rolls and won ton. "We're Jewish," he'd say: "We don't eat ham, bacon, or pork." That Don the Beachcomber's famous spare ribs, glistening on the tables of gentiles and sinful Jews around us, were taboo made me question the God of Israel. What did He have against spare ribs? And why, furthermore, did He not permit his chosen people to order Don the Beachcomber's greatest contribution to world gastronomy, the quintessential Hawaiian food — rumaki, a chicken liver and water chestnut wrapped in a piece of bacon, toothpick skewered, and deep fried?

I envied Christians who, for some reason, were apparently able to eat rumaki without suffering the wrath of God. I envied pagans even more, those idolatrous natives of Hawai'i as depicted in the posters, prints, and paintings on the walls of Don the Beachcomber's. They were, I surmised, allowed to eat anything they wanted. Hawaiian kids could drink flaming cocktails and freely gaze at beautiful babes who didn't cover their breasts with anything more than fragrant floral leis. Their god, Tiki, unlike our stern Lord, was a God of Fun. He didn't smite anyone, cause floods, or ever command His people to wander in a wilderness. He never forbade the eating of any of the fruit in the Eden of the Pacific. He knew what tasted good — things like rumaki. The menu proclaimed it "pupu of the gods."

I was grateful, however, that at least my father was religiously liberal enough to allow us to indulge ourselves, despite Levitical laws, in those ambrosial Kon Tiki Coconut Shrimp.

After everything but the flowers on the bountiful Polynesian Pupu Platter had been devoured, I'd order the Pipi Kola Steak and Pineapple Skewers. It was presented with a Tiki-pot of Sterno so that I could char the meat and caramelize the fruit to perfection. The only vegetable I liked at home was corn on the cob, but in Don the Beachcomber's Hawai'i even things that were good for you tasted good, dishes like saucy peapods with crispy toasted almonds and crunchy water chestnut morsels. And then came the gastronomically sensational Kona Kurry Puffs, Hanalei Crab, Lolo Lilokoi Lobster, coconut-crusted papaya-garnished mahimahi, sweet-and-sour pressed duck, and finally pineapple ice cream and coconut cake.

Everything was served on carved monkey pod platters, or in coconut, abalone, scallop, or giant clam shells. Hawaiians, I believed, really knew how to eat, not just what to eat, but how to decorate it. Without the pineapple slices, shredded coconut, and vanda blossoms, served on an ordinary ceramic plate, rather than in a shell, carved monkey pod bowl, or Tiki-pedestaled platter, the Hawaiian delicacies might have been mistaken for Chinese food.

My best friend in the fourth grade, Robbie Freeman, was no less an aficionado of Don the Beachcomber's Hawaiian cuisine than I. His parents not only took him to that restaurant, they also took him to Hawaiʻi. The islands weren't, Robbie dolefully confided, all they were cracked up to be. The girls did, in fact, wear tops, and, according to my pal, you couldn't get "real Hawaiian food" over there: "No, the food's really crappy. We went to a lūʻau and they served a lot of gooey purple-gray stuff called poi. It tastes like Elmer's glue. They cooked a pig in the ground — I'm not kidding — a whole pig with its hooves, eyes, tongue, tail, and even its balls still on it. Yeah, they buried it in the dirt with hot rocks, and they wrapped an old fish and some spinach in a soggy leaf and put that in the pit, too. And — you're not going to believe this, but I swear to God it's true — they don't even have Hawaiian Punch in Hawaiʻi."

Despite his disillusionment with the actual islands of the Pacific, Robbie maintained a dream of a Hawaiʻi more real than the real place. He convinced his mother to decorate their basement bomb shelter as a Hawaiian hut complete with grass matting on the walls, a large clam shell filled with fairly realistic wax tropical fruit, a rubber palm tree, Matson Line posters, and black plaster cast of a Tiki with ruby-red glass eyes. He had bought an ʻukulele in Hawaiʻi and avowed he was going to learn to play it when the Russians bombed Los Angeles. "There won't be much else to do for those many months that we'll be spending in our shelters until all the radioactive fallout is gone." The Freeman's shelter was, furthermore, enviably well stocked with industrial-size cans of Dole pineapple, jars of neon-red maraschino cherries, bags of toasted coconut chips, boxes of Mounds Bars (qualifying as Hawaiian because of the coconut), and gallons of Hawaiian Punch syrup mix. "At least I'll be eating and drinking well after the Commies drop the H-bomb on us."

Several years later Robbie was further able to coerce his parents into renting Kelbo's South Seas Restaurant for his Bar Mitzvah lūʻau party. He had wanted Don the Beachcomber's, but settled for Kelbo's because it was on Fairfax Boulevard within walking distance of the synagogue where the more tediously solemn liturgical part of the Jewish rite of passage would take place. The rabbi was Reform enough to consent to Robbie wearing an aloha shirt under his prayer shawl and a yarmulke his mother had made out of a Hawaiian floral patterned cloth. It looked like half a bikini top with its straps removed.

It was astounding to hear the leader of the Kelbo's Wiki Wacky Waikīkī Band play "Hava Nagila" on the 'ukulele.

Although genuine Hawaiian Punch, garnished with canned pineapple slices, Tiki stirring sticks, and paper umbrellas, was served (spiked with rum added for the adults), there was, in keeping with Jewish dietary laws, no pork nor shellfish on the menu. The Kelbo's chef had tried to pass off as Hawaiian Wilno kosher hot dogs, cut into bite-size pieces, skewered on toothpicks with pineapple bits, dipped in Hawaiian honey glaze, and served on a large gardenia- and hibiscus-strewn monkey pod platter. But I didn't buy it. No, for me, the one and only authentic Hawaiian cuisine was, and will forever be, that Kon Tiki Coconut Shrimp that I ate over fifty years ago at Don the Beachcomber's South Seas Restaurant on McCadden Place in Hollywood.

Lee Siegel is a professor of religion at the University of Hawai'i. He is the author of numerous works of non-fiction and fiction, including *Love in a Dead Language, Love and Other Games of Chance, Who Wrote the Book of Love?* and, most recently, *Love and the Incredibly Old Man.*

Questions to Tourists Stopped by the Pineapple Field

W.S. Merwin

Did you like your piece of pineapple   would you like a napkin
who gave you the pineapple   what do you know about them
do you eat much pineapple   where you come from
how did this piece compare   with pineapple you have eaten before
what do you remember about the last time   you ate a piece of pineapple
did you know where it came from   how much did it cost
do you remember the first time   you tasted pineapple
do you like it better fresh   or from the can
what do you remember   of the picture on the can
what did you feel   as you looked at the picture
which do you like better   the picture or the pineapple field
did you ever imagine   pineapples growing somewhere

how do you like   these pineapple fields
have you ever seen   pineapple fields before
do you know whether pineapple   is native to the islands
do you know whether the natives   ate pineapple
do you know whether the natives   grew pineapple
do you know how the land was acquired   to be turned into pineapple fields
do you know what is done to the land   to turn it into pineapple fields
do you know how many months   and how deeply they plow it
do you know what those machines do   are you impressed
do you know what's in those containers   are you interested

what do you think was here   before the pineapple fields
would you suppose that the fields   represent an improvement
do you think they smell better   than they did before
what is your opinion   of those square miles of black plastic
where do you think the plastic   goes when the crop is over
what do you think becomes of the land   when the crop is over
do you think the growers know best   do you think this is for your own good

what and where was the last   bird you noticed
do you remember   what sort of bird it was
do you know whether   there were birds here before
are there any birds   where you come from
do you think it matters   what do you think matters more
have you seen any   natives since you arrived
what were they doing   what were they wearing
what language were they speaking   were they in nightclubs
are there any natives   where you come from

have you taken pictures   of the pineapple fields
would you like for me   to hold the camera
so that you can all   be in the picture
would you mind   if I took your picture
standing in front   of those pineapple fields
do you expect   to come back

what made you decide   to come here
was this what   you came for
when did you first   hear of the islands
where were you then   how old were you
did you first see the islands   in black and white
what words were used   to describe the islands
what do the words mean   now that you are here
what do you do   for a living
what would you say is   the color of pineapple leaves
when you look at things in rows   how do you feel
would you like to dream   of pineapple fields

is this your first visit   how do you like the islands
what would you say   in your own words
you like best   about the islands
what do you want   when you take a trip
when did you get here   how long will you be staying
did you buy any clothes   especially for the islands
how much did you spend on them   before you came
was it easy to find clothes   for the islands
how much have you spent on clothes   since you got here
did you make your own plans   or are you part of a group
would you rather be on your own   or with a group
how many are in your group   how much was your ticket
are the side-tours part of the ticket   or are they extra
are hotel and meals and car   part of the ticket or extra
have you already paid   or will you pay later
did you pay by check   or by credit card
is this car rented   by the day or week
how does it compare   with the one you drive at home
how many miles   does it do to a gallon
how far do you   want to go on this island

where have you been   in the last three hours
what have you seen   in the last three miles
do you feel hurried   on your vacation
are you getting   your money's worth
how old are you   are you homesick are you well
what do you eat here   is it what you want
what gifts are you planning   to take back
how much do you expect   to spend on them
have you decided   where to put each thing
what will you say   about where they came from
what will you say   about the pineapple fields

do you like dancing here   what do you do when it rains
was this trip   purely for pleasure
do you drink more   or less than at home
how do you like   the place where you live now
were you born there   how long have you lived there
what does the name mean   is it a growth community
why are you living there   how long do you expect to stay
how old is your house   would you like to sell it

in your opinion   coming from your background
what do the islands offer   someone of your age
are there any changes   you would like to promote
would you like to invest here   would you like to live here
if so would it be year round   or just for part of the year
do you think there is a future   in pineapple

The Chicharon Widows

Amalia B. Bueno

Everybody knows Margarita Corpuz and Estrelita Salvador. They always come on Sundays. They wake up at five a.m. when it's still dark to bake popular desserts like bibingka, tupig, and puto. Then they pick and pack their homegrown vegetables. They fry pork rinds just before loading up their big, baby blue Ford truck. By the time they pull inside the yellow gates with its FRESH SHRIMP sign, it's already 7:15, when most of the breeders and cockfighters have already unloaded and set up for the day.

Margarita and Estrelita, also called "the chicharon widows," and also known as The RitaLitas, have been coming to the cockfights for two years now. Rita told me once the House considers them regulars. But they were not regular long enough, she said, to be on the "guarantee same spot list." She had added with a shrug, "Our spot could be better, but dis good enough. Going get plenny people who see us," was her philosophy. Today the widows are set up three lanes away from the main cockpit, a coveted spot that is guaranteed to bring in lots of foot traffic.

I greet them in their booth, where a sign advertising "RitaLita's Famous Chicharon" is prominent. The white script lettering and comic rendering of dancing chicharon in browns and yellows hangs sturdy just inside the food booth's blue tarp covering. You would have to be blind to miss the sign's animated smiling pork rinds, hands joined with alternating yellow plumeria and red hibiscus flowers. The dancing legs of the happy chicharon and aloha-print clad tropical flowers point to the letters in the middle. Their appendages surround the words RitaLita's Famous Chicharon like a lei. It was almost tacky, save for the feelings it evoked of warm kitchens, pleasant fragrances, and happy childhoods.

Rita, the primary namesake, is dressed in a long-sleeved blue chambray work shirt and is milling around under the sign. Her sleeves are rolled up to her elbows and expose strong arms and calloused, veined hands. Her hands are Ilocano hands — big and strong. Her fingers knobby, the kind that are accustomed to digging into the fertile earth of Laoag, Ilocos Norte, where her family is from. Her business partner, Lita, is helping a slightly plump teen-age girl pick out some desserts from a wooden display rack. Lita wears a calabash gourd hard hat. Her Army green fatigues are tucked into black rubber boots splashed with just-as-famous, red Waialua mud. I wave to both of the widows.

Their vegetable bounty is piled on three tables pushed together in a U and arrayed like a harvest cornucopia. The bright colors of the vegetables compete with the intense hues of the tablecloth, dyed with characteristic vivid stripes and patterns of native ikat weavers. Karabasa, or kabocha as the Hapons call it, take up most of the space. The mottled green and yellow-streaked pumpkins are tight-skinned and fecund, like pregnant globes. Long, dark green, snake beans are bunched together by the pound and tied with raffia. Their slender bean bodies form graceful curves, nestled and piled on top of each other. Next to them are patani, wing beans large and small that are neatly sorted by size and fitted into quart ZipLock bags. Eggplant, singkamas, sweet potatoes, green chili peppers for dinuguan, squash for sari-sari. Kamatis, laya, bawang, sibuyas — tomatoes, ginger, garlic, onions. It is a vegetable stew on the tables.

Then there are the leaves. Paria shoots with small yellow flowers, saluyot greens bereft of their slimy okra fruit. Camote, sayote, and marunggay with its splayed canopy of foliage. Lush kangkong propped up on its hollow reed stems.

Then there are the flowers, carefully placed in the shady area of the table so they won't wilt. There are beautiful, still-closed tabungao flower buds, nowadays filled with fancy items and fried by gourmet chefs to be called something high makamaka like sautéed squash blossoms stuffed with crumbled feta and pine nuts. I move past three women who are picking through a stack of white, curved, beak-shaped flowers and putting the choice ones in their plastic bags. The Filipino name of this flower eludes me, but I visualize a white flower salad with tomatoes and patis.

My favorite vegetable, kabatiti, is stacked in a tall woven basket. I can never remember what this vegetable is called in English. When I first saw kabatiti as a child they reminded me of dinosaurs. They still do today as I pick one up and see a brontosaurus with its slim neck and elongated, fleshy body. I run my pointer along the hard, green ridges that run the entire length of its back. I smile at the two, good-sized ones I have captured in my hand and make them face each other. Looking around to see if anyone is watching, I bring the dinosaurs into mock battle. Gently though, so their small-tipped heads don't get knocked off like my brother and I used to do as children on my lola's kitchen table. When one head got toppled, it signaled the end of the fight.

Then I see something new. I cannot believe it. It is ingenious entrepreneurship at its best. I marvel at how the chicharon widows are always looking out for their customers. I pick up a bag of the new item.

"Dass for young ladies like you. I make es-pe-shall for your kind," says Rita, walking over toward me and her creation. "Nowadays people no more time for cook. Always go outside and eat. Go out, go out, all the time go outside to eat. Like my son and his family. I don't know why his wife no like cook."

Maybe she's tired like me after a long day at work, I silently respond in my head. But I just smile. Rita looks me straight in the eye. "Dat one in your hands. Dat going help you make good Filipino food for your family."

We both look at the plastic ZipLock bag filled with all of the pre-cut, pre-sorted, pre-layered fixings you would ever need to make pinakbet. You would have to just simply unzip the bag and pour. This is exactly what my generation needs. Pinakbet 101. Pinakbet Helper. Fast Stovetop Pinakbet.

"How old you now? Around thirty-two, yeah? You no more children, hah?" she asks, slightly accusatory and sounding like a social commentary on the sad state of small nuclear family units.

"No, Nana. But I have plenty nieces and nephews, so the bloodline will continue," I reply. I count on her not noticing my accompanying smirk, as it would definitely be a sign of disrespect.

"Dass good, dass good. Your younger sister is good she has her own family. How many kids now? Four? Her husband come from big family, too. The children can help. They can all help each other."

"You know how to make dis?" she asks about the bag I am holding in my hands. I give her a tentative facial expression, a cross between discomfort and eagerness. I try to nod a yes, but she senses my hesitation and takes the bag from my fingers.

"I show you how. First, like dis." She pulls the top open and fishes out the first layer. She retrieves a large pot from under the table. I am amazed again at how ready the widows are for anything. They could probably feed a crowd at a moment's notice with nothing but a five-pound box of chicken in their freezer.

"Cook the ginger and tomato with water. See the ginger? Already smashed, so no need do that. Next layer is the big cherry tomatoes I put inside. So no need chop. Here's the onions next. Stay in big pieces already, so no need cut. Then add the water and the bugguong and then you boil. You get bugguong at home? Every house get. You get some, hah?

I furnish her with a definitive nod, but it is a lie. I don't have any bugguong. I have imported patis in a bottle I bought from 99 Ranch in … I think it was 1999. I keep it in the refrigerator. The expiration date has probably passed. I wonder if patis even has an expiration date. It's already fermented, so how can it rot some more?

"How much water do I put inside, Nana?" I ask.

Rita pauses. "You don't know?" She responds wide-eyed, incredulous at such an innocent question. "How come you don't know how to cook dis one? What kind Filipina you?"

I answer her in my head, the kind that don't know how to cook pinakbet.

"How come you don't know how? Aye, every Filipina should know. You watch your mama and your lola make pinakbet, hah."

There's nothing I can do but shrug. I am guilty of not watching my elders cook. I know Rita means well, but I am feeling more and more intimidated the longer I remain in her presence. Her three daughters — Perla, Myrna, and Rona — must have had it tough growing up female in her household. Her eldest, Perla, was my classmate at Hale'iwa Elementary School. Perla was not someone teachers would remember as a happy-go-lucky child. With a mother like Nana Rita, I now understand why Perla was a quiet, serious, straight A student who seldom smiled.

Rita sighs as she answers my question about how much water to use. "You put enough water to cover the tomatoes. This much," she says as she pours water into the pot. The woman has made water appear out of nowhere.

"Just enough water, but not too much. Or else going get mushy. And don't stir. Don't do dis." She makes an exaggerated stirring motion with a ladle, which she has also magically produced from air, to demonstrate. "Just keep putting everything on top. Every kind stay inside the bag already. Next comes this."

She pours out cubed, bite-sized pumpkin squares. "Next comes this one." Out tumble three-inch pieces of shiny, purple eggplant. "But you have to soak first. No forget now. Soak the tarong to get the bitterness out. You soak in water for five minutes."

I am terrified to ask how much water I need to soak the eggplant.

Rita continues to demonstrate with each layer, diminishing the contents of the ZipLock bag. Long beans, ends trimmed and snapped in even lengths. Wing beans, the small ones cut and the larger ones shelled for their spotted, flat fruit, which are added as another layer. I can almost smell it cooking. Next is the okra, then the kabatiti. There is a deep slit in each rectangle piece. Sequa, that's what it's called in English, I remember. And silk squash. And Chinese okra. Of all the stupid things to liken kabatiti to is okra. It's like the kiwi being called a Chinese gooseberry.

"See dis? You cut kabatiti like dis so all the flavors can go inside. I saw you looking at the kabatiti over there. You can make good soup with dis, too. You take some chicken or pork with dis one here. Aysus, broke da mouth. I no understand why you young people go eat outside alla time."

"You can cut like dis, too. Into stars, see? Thick like dis." Rita demonstrates with a small paring knife she makes appear, again out of nowhere. The sliced medallions look like flat suns with multi-pointed sunbeams. I guess it could look like stars.

"And if you no more meat, you just stir fry dis one only and stay ono by itself. Dis is good, stay easy and stay fast. Dis one good vegetable." She pronounces vegetable in four syllables. Ve-je-tah-bull. Just like my mom used to. Ve-je-tah-bull.

"You cover everything. And you cook until finish." I prepare for the worst, but decide to ask anyway.

"And for how long you cook, Nana?"

She shakes her head. "You can see, hah? You open the pot and look. You cook until it's pau! You taste, then you look inside again." She retrieves a pot cover from beneath the tablecloth and fits it on the pot. "Then you taste again. Don't overcook. You cover and toss all the ve-je-tah-bulls. You just toss like this so the bottom layer come to the top. You wait leelah bit, then you toss again," she instructs, pantomiming a gentle tossing motion using the pot's side handles.

The lesson is over because the pinakbet is done. Rita wipes her hands on her pants, and then places them on her hips. She wags a pointer near my face. "Remember the secret. Don't stir. It's easy once you know how." Finally, she smiles at me. I am encouraged. I feel like I could actually make pinakbet like she did.

"You make it look really easy, Nana," I say as I help her retrieve the contents from the pot and return them to the bag that I am going to buy. "Dios ti agngina. Nana." I can still remember the phrases that leave an impression of a decent Ilocano upbringing. She seems pleased at this.

"Wait, wait, wait. Don't forget the chicharon. Put the chicharon last. And wait leelah while before you eat. So dat all the flavors go inside the meat." I nod and spy their famous product on the table to my left, where Lita is arranging the bags on three, tiered planks supported by decorative cement blocks.

"Hoy, Bolo! Whatchoo doin' hea so early? Plenny fish today?" Rita calls out to the bolohead man driving his black SUV past their booth. The man slows down, pulls over, gets out, and starts walking toward us. Bolo usually comes around lunchtime to sell poke. It's no secret that his poke is the best because of the freshness of his fish. The raw flesh is always shiny and creamy.

"I helping my friend with his chicken today, manang. My wife going come bring the poke bumbye," Bolo explains to Rita.

I walk toward the chicharon and Lita, who greets me with "Kumusta, balasang ko." I respond properly. She offers to take my pinakbet ingredients, kabatiti brontosauruses, and sweet potato tops while I look over the desserts and pork rinds.

Lita is the behind-the-scenes person of their successful operation. Rita and Lita lived together and acted like they were sisters, but they were actually sisters-in-law. Rita had the green thumb, but it was Lita who made the pork rinds. I wonder why Rita's name came first on the label. Maybe it was because Rita was the older one. Maybe it was Rita's idea. Then I remembered why.

When my mother was still alive, she was known for keeping up with the latest tsismis, and was a popular resource for all of the juicy Waialua Town gossip. It was common knowledge that Rita's parents had been trying very hard to get her married off, but Rita refused their suggestions for a potential husband. It was local folklore that Rita was nearly thirty years old when she married her cousin's cousin, Danilo Corpuz, from her clan's neighboring village of Isabela. Danilo became a truck driver for Dole Pineapple Company by day. During his free time he raised fighting cocks as a hobby. Rita sold vegetables and desserts as a side business on cockfight days. I heard my mom tell my dad that the Corpuz family was getting rich on Danilo's chickens and Rita's bibingka.

At the height of their success Mr. Corpuz died unexpectedly of a stroke. Rita was left with five young children — three girls and two boys — to raise on her own. At the funeral mass Padre Pinacate said that Danilo was a hard-working man, a decent man, a good man who did not mind having a strong-headed wife. I never forgot that because the congregation laughed after he said it. To make a long story short, Rita ended up marrying her husband's younger brother, Lito, who volunteered to step in for his brother, according to traditional custom. Rita's children needed a father and Lito wanted to come to Hawai'i and become an American.

Years later Lito was eventually able to bring his mother, father, three sisters, two brothers-in-law, four nieces, and six nephews from the Philippines. Their household grew into an extended family, which needed an expanded houselot. There are five homes now on the Corpuz family compound. Lito's youngest sister, Lita, was the last to arrive from the Philippines.

Here's the part that gets interesting. Rita's brother, Perfecto, ended up marrying Lita, her husband's sister. This was because Perfecto's wife had died of breast cancer a couple of years after Lita arrived. Perfecto was left a widower with seven children. Lita stepped in to marry him, just as her brother Lito had done for Rita ten years earlier. Lita was twenty. Perfecto was forty-five. The gossip was that the Corpuz family wanted to pay Rita's family back for helping to bring them to America. They wanted to show gratitude for ending up with a better life in Hawai'i. The arrangement was a bit chaotic and strange, but in the end it worked out. Rita and Lita are both widows now, with all their children and stepchildren grown.

Lita's husband, Apo Perfecto, as we children called him back then, didn't get involved with raising chickens. But he was a regular at cockfights and knew what he was doing as a gambler. He would follow the progress of all the breeders and the fighting cocks and was personable to all. He did not like it when the newer breeders began using steroids. This seemed unfair to him, so he made a big stink about it. He knew which breeders were shooting up the cocks right before a big fight. As a respected elder, he tried talking to the younger breeders and hoped they would understand the older, traditional ways of the sport and its protocol. At first the young breeders demurred and were semi-committed to fighting clean, but eventually they ignored him altogether. The practice of using steroids continued to spread and it greatly bothered him.

Apo Perfecto took the issue to the House and asked them to intervene by banning the use of steroids; they did not. The House leadership did not consider this touchy subject a part of their kuleana, so they let it go on. Apo Perfecto tried to convince them that the sport was not only about making money. But it was to no avail. In his frustration, he gave up cockfighting and concentrated on drinking.

With Lita's husband's new pastime making him a bitter and crotchety old man, she found herself raising his children alone. There were rumors of him being an abusive father, so Lita took to his children as if they were her own blood relations. After her husband died of liver failure, Lita began selling chicharon out of her home on Sundays. Shortly after that, RitaLita's Famous Chicharon was born and they took it to the Sunday cockfights instead. It is now a best best seller at cockfights in Waialua, · Wai'anae, and Waipahu. Southern Cross Stores in Kalihi sells it exclusively.

"You don't have any of the hard kind today," I point out to Lita, who was straightening out a row of bags on the other end of the planks.

"No more already. I just sell the last five bags to Bolo. Everybody like the old-fashioned way, with the fat on the inside. I save some for you next week if you like," Lita says brusque and efficient.

"And these soft, fluffy ones. How you make them so light, Nana?"

"Ah, you have to dry that one in the sun. And you poke holes on the hard side of the skin. The Puerto Ricans and the haoles like that kind. You use pork belly, not pork back. And you use hot, hot oil to fry in. Use only the skin. No meat. No fat."

"And what about these ones?" I pick up a bag that contained tender meat and moist fat topped off by a blistered, crackling thin layer of skin. It was mostly meat like Chinese roast pork but drier. I hadn't quite noticed the subtle differences among the contents of the bags before. I did notice they were sealed with twist ties of different colors. ZipLock bags would make them lose their crunchiness, I presumed.

"That's our new one. Meed-jum. Soft for the haoles. Hard for the Filipinos. And meed-jum for everybody else," Lita explained. Now I know why the RitaLita's were so successful. They adapted to changing needs. They worked hard. They gave from the heart all the time.

"How you make them hard, Nana?"

"You dry in the sun inside the screen box. Or hang up on the clothesline. Or on top the tray inside the oven. Then you fry slow, not so fast and noisy. So the skin no break up. You use pork back, not pork belly."

For all of the RitaLita's culinary secrets, they sure were easy about sharing them. I did not expect tough, enterprising widows to be so generous. It seemed easy enough to make these famous pork rinds. I am going to ask Mrs. Bautista to try to copy it. An old, authentic hand like Mrs. Bautista would be able to duplicate the soft, medium, and hard varieties with the information I had already gleaned from the widows. I could then trade what I knew about the RitaLita's recipe for Mrs. Bautista's dinuguan recipe. The one she makes with the mild peppers in her version of pork blood stew. The Bautistas might want to add pork rinds to their repertoire of Filipino plate lunch offerings, fresh hot corn, and fried lumpia they offered at the Bautista's Best food booth.

I could propose different flavored pork rids to Mrs. Bautista. Barbecue flavor. Ranch dressing flavor. Basalmic vinegar flavor. Maybe sprinkle some li hing powder. Li hing pork rinds. Interesting. Or chili powder. Rinds fried in extra virgin olive oil. Pizza flavor. Taco flavor. The marketing possibilities were endless.

"Do you have a secret recipe, Nana?"

"And what you like know all that for? How come you asking all these kind questions?" a sharp voice behind me cuts into my reverie. Rita had been standing there all this time. She is sticking labels on bags of chicharon she pulls out from a large box. She looks at Lita and they exchange mysterious glances.

"Recipe? You like one recipe," Rita spits the word like it is a disgusting taste in her mouth. "Maria Conchita Peralta, for all the years I know you and your family, you never, ever been interested in the Filipino culture. And es-pe-shally the Filipino food. Why you like know now about this kind for?"

Rita is now directly in front of me, her face close to mine. "What you doing, Conchita? Spying on us? Or you all of a sudden became one born-again Filipina?"

She and Lita laugh heartily at this. I have to laugh, too. It is Lita who laughs so hard tears start rolling down her cheeks. She seems to be enjoying a really good inside joke.

"I want to collect authentic Filipino recipes, Nana. I want to put them together in a cookbook. I cannot find any cookbooks in Hawai'i about Filipino food."

"Chita, you joking, hah?" Lita catches her breath from laughing and leans in toward me. "What I need one recipe for? I know how to make already!" It is Lita's turn to make fun of me.

"I no give out my recipe to anybody. Not even my children know how to make chicharon like me. They ask me alla time to write it down. I tell them you come watch and learn. But they no like. They only like me make more money. They tell me to sell my recipe. Santa Maria! I not gonna do dat. I gonna take this recipe with me to my grave."

"This is something we no share," Lita concludes. "You young people better watch out. Nobody going know how to make this kind food any more."

Rita nods. "I tell you this if you really like do something about keeping the tradition. I give you one hint. We use red Hawaiian salt. The kind from Kaua'i in the salt ponds. Another important secret is when you fry, you fry with the cover on."

"Here, take this. This is the hard kind we save for es-pe-shall people," Rita continues and hands a bag of her backup stash to me.

"Now, with all that we told you, you can try to make your chicharon like this. You can try make it better than ours. You can try real hard, but it's RitaLita's secret. I can guarantee you that yours not going taste like ours."

That was the most I could get out of the chicharon widows. Armed with a bag each of soft, medium, and hard chicharon, I go to find Bino Bautista at the payut tent. I have my heart set on impressing him.

Amalia B. Bueno's poetry and fiction has been published by Bamboo Ridge, Meritage Press, Our Own Voice, Katipunan Journal, and Mutual Publishing. Her work is forthcoming in anthologies by Spinster Ink Press (*Women. Period*) and Philippine American Literary House (*Growing Up Filipino*). She is currently working on a play, *The Four Maria Claras*.

Food and Friends

Catherine E. Toth

There was no question about it. My girlfriend had, in a surprise move, quit her high-paying job in Hawai'i, rented out a two-bedroom apartment she had just renovated, and moved to Reno. In the middle of winter.

Yes, it sounded crazy. But love — and she was well in it — has a reputation for encouraging people to do crazy things. In this case, move to Reno without a job during a blizzard.

So when I heard she was coming home after four months of living out of cardboard boxes and working at a small print shop — which, to make matters worse, was going out of business — it was obvious what we needed to do.

Eat.

And probably with the option of margaritas.

There's something about food — especially during highly emotional times, whether dealing with a bad break-up or moving 2,500 miles away from a decent sushi bar — that provides the only comfort for that pang of pain and suffering.

When I lived in Chicago for a year attending graduate school — a ten-hour plane ride from Honolulu and at least twenty degrees colder — I had to bring along what I considered staples to survival: several cans of SPAM, a bottle of furikake, a few packages of kakimochi and, of course, a five-cup rice cooker.

Food is such an integral part of living in Hawai'i. It's the focal point of any gathering, from traditional baby lū'aus to local-style weddings to corporate retreats. If you don't have good food, don't bother.

But it often takes large-scale, highly planned get-togethers for my friends and me to ever see each other anymore.

Since turning thirty — and that wasn't recently — I've become too busy to do much more than work and sleep. Even eating has become an abbreviated experience. Everything is quick, fast, right now. I'm driving from an early morning surf session directly to work, stopping at Jack in the Box for a ninety-nine-cent chicken sandwich and a large Diet Coke. On my way to meetings, I'll grab a handful of stale pretzels in the office and call that lunch. If Kozo Sushi and W&M Burger had drive-thru windows, I'd be the next spokesperson for Jenny Craig.

And it's true with all my friends, especially those with kids who often resort to eating their children's leftovers or crusts from peanut butter and jelly sandwiches to satisfy their lunch cravings.

But it wasn't always like that. Despite outward appearances, there was a time when eating was central to our friendships.

In high school we ate at the same table in the cafeteria, swapping bread rolls and complementing the dreaded hamburger patty with a SPAM musubi we bought earlier from 7-Eleven. This is when we connected, chatting incessantly, deconstructing the outfits of fellow classmates, and predicting the next prom royalty.

Then in college we'd meet at every break between classes possible, whether to grab a blended coffee drink or a two-dollar taco.

It's as if food — whether a bucket of fried chicken or a platter of gooey nachos — drove our conversation and fueled our friendship. We almost didn't have one without the other.

Even now, in between nursing newborns and juggling two jobs, my girlfriends will meet up if there's food involved. Weddings, birthday parties, baby showers, even funerals — we seem able to justify adjusting our already busy schedules and make time to see each other in the PDAs we can't seem to find.

So when our newly unemployed, parka-wearing girlfriend was back in town, it wasn't difficult for the rest of us to reschedule yoga classes and find babysitters to meet up for an appetizer sampler and a round of drinks.

The only challenge, really, was deciding on a place to eat.

And my girlfriend, who was already craving something other than chain restaurants, had a few requests: The restaurant had to serve fish — preferably in raw form — and sticky rice. And, of course, a decent selection of alcoholic beverages.

So after a round of e-mails — most of which included the phrase, "Can't wait to see everyone! It's been so long!" — we decided on Sam Choy's Breakfast Lunch & Crab, a local eatery and microbrewery in the industrial area of Iwilei. This restaurant, which opened in 1997, has long been known for its fresh fish dishes — including a wok-seared poke appetizer that I'd miss, too, if I were stuck in Reno — its very local flavors, and the kind of casual atmosphere that doesn't require uncomfortable shoes.

As I've gotten older, I've come to adopt a different set of standards for restaurants. It's become less about the scene and more about the menu — and how long the manager will let us sit at our table and laugh obnoxiously loud.

We started with appetizers — coconut-breaded shrimp, marinated shoyu poke, golden-fried calamari with horseradish ketchup — and opted for li hing margaritas as our main entrée. Because as much as the food matters — we raved about the grilled kālua pork quesadilla with sautéed onions and melted cheese for a full two minutes — the company mattered more. And this company wouldn't have met over soggy tortilla chips and badly executed eggplant Parmesan.

As I sat around our table, I realized something: aside from our far-flung girlfriend, we all live within — literally — a two-mile radius. And yet we haven't seen each other in months. It took someone visiting from Reno — and the promise of fresh poke and microbrewed beer — to bring us together.

And you know, armed with a margarita and a good laugh about moving a queen-size bed in the snow, even that didn't matter much.

Catherine E. Toth is a free-lance writer and blogger based in Honolulu. A former staff writer at *The Honolulu Advertiser*, she covered everything from relationships to college football, small business to ABC's "The Bachelor." When she's not working — or writing — she can be found somewhere in the Pacific Ocean, surfboard in tow.

cane haul road ltd.

cat and musubi

Poke:
A Recent Culinary Tradition

Kristin M. McAndrews

On Maui, thirty-two years ago, at a Hawaiian first birthday lū'au, I tasted poke for the first time. I had been a visitor in Hāna for one week. The host led me to a huge buffet table spread with many foods I had never seen before. He scooped a rather substantial helping of poke on my plate along with a small, raw blue crab and a couple of raw marinated 'opihi. He also handed me some chopsticks. Thankfully, I was adept at chopsticks, but I had never eaten raw fish before. The fishy, seaweedy flavors and the crunchy but soft texture of the poke shocked my mouth. Further, I was stunned to find that I needed to eat the entire raw crab, shell and all. As my host stood by, I ate politely, trying to minimize my facial expressions at the new tastes and textures.

Many years later, I became interested in the role of food in relationship to the popular culture of Hawai'i. One early afternoon, I sat at Kaimana Beach in Waikīkī, watching my son play in the waves. I am not sure why but I noticed a variety of people eating poke — out of plastic or paper containers — with plastic forks or chopsticks. After walking down the beach snooping a bit, I could see people eating different varieties of poke. Also, the poke diners seemed to be local residents from Hawai'i rather than visitors.

Poke is a more recent food tradition rather than a practice based on traditions of old Hawai'i. The Hawaiian dictionary defines poke, "to slice, cut crosswise into pieces, as fish or wood; to press out as the meat of an 'opihi shell; section, slice." In other words, poke does not refer to the fish dish itself. In her extensive study of Hawaiian cuisine, Rachel Lauden notes that in accounts of Hawaiian uses of fish and the first ethnic cookbooks, there is no mention of poke as a fish dish. Nor does the Hawaiian dictionary or the major glossary of pidgin have references to poke as a fish dish.

The Hawaiian liking for raw food is also absent from many anthropological accounts of the Hawaiian people. One historian claims that Native Hawaiian people rarely ate raw fish or meat, and when they did it was only out of necessity. John Wise says, "They [the Native Hawaiians] always dried it or preserved it in some way before eating it." Yet, at traditional Native Hawaiian lūʻaus numerous raw foods are presented, from limpets, fish, and crab to marinated pig's liver. Sometime during the early 1970s poke became an appetizer to eat with a beer or bring to a party — only since the mid-1970s have recipes been recorded. In 1998, when I interviewed Hari Kojima, a former cooking show host (Hari's Kitchen), he claimed responsibility for poke's increased cross-cultural popularity.

These days poke is loosely translated to mean a Hawaiian marinated dish of raw, seared, or cooked seafood (and sometimes tofu). In other words, poke is a relative newcomer to the local culinary market. In 1999, Sam Choy (Hawaiʻi Regional Cuisine chef) published *Sam Choy's Poke: Hawaiian Soul Food*. The collection represents winning recipes from the poke contest at the Big Island Poke Festival. As reflected in Choy's cookbook title, poke is sometimes referred to as Hawaiʻi's soul food. One can make it at home, buy it in a fish market or grocery store, and order it in a local eatery, from high-profile Hawaiʻi Regional Cuisine restaurants to the local fast-food place.

Actually, while an acquired taste, poke's popularity has spread to the continental United States. I have seen mahimahi and salmon poke offered at seafood restaurants in Seattle, San Francisco, Monterey, and Los Angeles. Sam Choy travels around the United States to food festivals sharing poke recipes. He might argue that a soft white fish, should be used for ceviche-like recipes rather than for poke. A firm red fish like raw tuna (ʻahi or aku) makes a delicious poke. Recently in Paris, I had a poisson tartare that resembled poke — raw sea bass, salmon, ground almonds, seaweed, and sesame oil.

While hundreds of variations exist, traditional poke and shoyu poke are the most popular in Hawaiʻi. Traditional poke is typically made of raw ʻahi (tuna), limu aliʻi or limu kohu (seaweed), ʻalaea (large-grained salt), and roasted ʻinamona (ground kukui nut). Traditional poke is often available in fish markets rather than in grocery stores, in part because the indigenous seaweeds and kukui nuts are considered specialty items — difficult to get, thus expensive. The most popular style of poke is shoyu poke, often made with raw ʻahi, Hawaiian salt, sesame oil, ogo (aqua-cultured seaweed), chili pepper, shoyu, and chopped white and green onions.

At fish markets and grocery stores, poke is usually served in a plastic container or a paper bowl and eaten with chopsticks.

Alan Young, a second-generation owner of Young's Fish Market told me that many people buy a bowl of rice or poi with a dish of poke, making it a complete meal. At upscale restaurants, the poke presentation is more complex, such as Alan Wong's (Hawai'i Regional Cuisine chef) poke-pines. Chopped poke is covered with thin noodle dough shaped to look like a pineapple. They are quickly deep-fried and served on a plate decorated with a wasabi-soy mélange, some chopped pink ginger, and thinly grated white horseradish. Chopsticks or forks are offered as implements for this dish. Poke can be eaten any time, but typically it is served as a snack, lunch, or an appetizer.

With poke's popularity, it is no wonder that the Poke Festival, in cooperation with Aloha Festivals, celebrates this new, yet traditional dish. Aloha Festivals honor Hawaiian and local folk culture by focusing on crafts or foods specific to Hawai'i's diverse ethnic culture. The three hundred-event festival celebrates Hawaiian heritage and local traditions and attracts both Mainland tourists and local people throughout the state. It is the only statewide festival in the United States, lasting for six weeks. The loss of cultural and ethnic traditions concerns many people who live in Hawai'i. Michael Largey, a specialist in music and culture, points out "tradition is formed in the present from evidence, perceptions, and impressions of the past. Tradition also uses images that imbue history with power, bringing the past into a relationship with the present." Aloha Festivals mediate the traditional cultural practice of Native Hawaiians with other ethnic and cultural groups established in Hawai'i.

The Poke Festival, held on the Big Island of Hawai'i in mid-September, is an annual celebration of poke. In 1992, Sam Choy started the Poke Festival, hosting a poke contest in a large tent in Waimea on the Big Island. As the contest grew in participants, the celebration moved to the Hāpuna Beach Prince Hotel and now incorporates cash and prizes, cooking classes, poke sampling, and a charity golf tournament. The festival has held poke contests with up to ninety entries. Presentations include creative visual displays that incorporate simple or complex poke recipes. Local and national politics, local traditions, and ethnic pride are reflected in the displays. Sometimes the presentations are humorous in context, consciously making fun of our culturally diverse community as well as images of popular culture. When I asked Glorianna Akau from

Aloha Festivals about the humor of some of the poke contest displays, she said, "If you can't laugh with one another then it's a hard job." The Poke Festival is a site for understanding how community creates itself and has fun doing it.

Kristin M. McAndrews, an associate professor of English at the University of Hawai'i, has lived in Hawai'i for thirty-two years. Her scholarship focuses on folklore and storytelling in relationship to culture and cuisine, tourism and gender.

The Dishes Have Evolved, the Flavors Are Still the Same

Joan Namkoong

In the last two decades, food in Hawai'i has changed in innumerable ways, a result of diversified agriculture, an efficient long-line fishery, celebrity chefs, fine-dining restaurants, a global economy, and our greater awareness of food and trends throughout the world. Our cuisine has evolved from the simple flavors and concepts of the traditional Hawaiian table and our humble plantation-era past to a contemporary cuisine that appeals to sophisticated palates. Yet in some ways, it has not changed at all.

In 1988, Roy's Restaurant opened in Hawai'i Kai, a benchmark event in Hawai'i's food history. Roy Yamaguchi's Euro-Asian blend of ingredients and cooking techniques, now characterized as Hawaiian fusion, brought a different sensibility to our taste buds. There was blackened 'ahi, a takeoff of Japanese 'ahi tataki, a seared-on-the-outside block of fish, seasoned with Yamaguchi's own Cajun-inspired spice blend that included a hint of sandalwood, served with a Colman mustard soy sauce dip reminiscent of Chinese chop suey houses.

Yamaguchi introduced us to traditional French beurre blanc sauces flavored with watercress and ginger or spiked with shichimi togarashi (seven spice chili blend) or rayu (spicy sesame oil). His cooking style was a marriage of bold Asian flavors with the subtle sauces of France and a melding of cooking techniques that revolutionized what we liked to eat and how we defined delicious.

A few years later, Yamaguchi and eleven other European- and American-trained chefs touted a new brand of cuisine: Hawai'i Regional Cuisine. These chefs brought about changes in agriculture and the fishing industry, utilized locally produced and harvested foods on their menus, and enhanced their creations with a wide range of herbs, spices, and flavorings that represented the many ethnic groups that had come to settle in Hawai'i. These chefs creatively tweaked the humble foods and flavors of the varied ethnic cultures that link us to our past and set us on a fun, flavorful, and exciting food adventure.

Take poke, the traditional ancient Hawaiian dish of bite-sized fish, ʻinamona (ground kukui nut), salt, and seaweed. It wasn't until the 1970s that poke began its life as a popular chaser for a cold beer. Today poke has taken on so many new flavors and incarnations. ʻAhi has become the fish of choice for this dish but tako, crab, mussels, clams, other fish, and even tofu have become the basis for poke.

Shoyu has become a key flavor ingredient for poke, not to mention ginger, garlic, wasabi, sesame oil, sweet onions, even mayonnaise, and chili sauces like sambal oelek, ko chu jang, and sriracha. Poke is still mostly raw, though fried poke has its own stature. Then there's the fried poke musubi, a creation of Chef Wayne Hirabayashi at the Kāhala Hotel, a crisp fried furikake-coated rice ball encasing ʻahi shoyu poke, a fine example of how we marry the flavors of Hawaiʻi's many ethnic peoples.

Kālua pig, another traditional Hawaiian food, has become a key ingredient in so many dishes today, loved for its smoky flavor and tenderness. It's paired with cheese in a tortilla for kālua pig quesadillas, used as a filling in fried spring rolls, wontons, and potstickers, added to risotto, or Caesar salad. Kālua pig is a staple of island chefs who are always finding new flavor combinations.

And then there's taro, the most sacred of foods for Native Hawaiians, a food that has become a part of our modern-day food repertoire in less than traditional ways. Poi, the starchy paste achieved by pounding the steamed taro corm and the starch staple of ancient Hawaiʻi, has become the basis for vinaigrettes and sauces in some of Hawaiʻi's top dining rooms. Cooked taro is used like potatoes to form a hash with bacon and onions, mashed like potatoes with milk and butter, pureed into soups, and even fried into crisp wafers for a crunchy snack, a foundation for delectable bite-sized morsels or a beautiful garnish.

It's truly amazing to see how simple butter-based and cream sauces of the Western kitchen have morphed into unique island sauces. Beurre blanc is the basic French butter sauce, a reduction of wine, vinegar, and shallots to which lots of butter is added. In Hawaiʻi Regional Cuisine, soy sauce was the first ingredient to be blended into beurre blanc. Then came Chinese fermented black beans, wasabi, lemon grass, garlic, ginger, sesame seeds and oil, curry, miso, tobiko, watercress, yuzu, passion fruit, mango, and many other ingredients that add pungent flavor mellowed by the richness of the butter. Who would have thought that this blending of delicate butter with tropical and Asian flavors would become de rigueur in restaurants throughout the state?

Cream sauces, loved for their velvety texture and richness, have changed, too, with the addition of a similar variety of ingredients. Or, the cream has been replaced with coconut milk, adding another measure of richness with an underlying flavor of our Pacific heritage.

There are some ingredients that punctuate contemporary food in surprising ways. Wasabi, Japanese horseradish, is one such ingredient, though rarely used in its fresh form. The more ubiquitous powdered form is mixed with a little water to form a green paste that packs a fiery bite between rice and seafood in sushi cuisine. In the islands, wasabi has become a unique flavor in mashed potatoes, butter and cream sauces, mayonnaise, and salad dressings.

And then there's li hing mui, the sweet sour, salty star anise combination that reminds many of us of small kid days when after school snack time meant a trip to the crack seed store. Li hing mui, traveler's plum, is the quintessential island flavor that has now been elevated to gourmet status. Chef Alan Wong of Alan Wong's Restaurant, created a li hing mui vinaigrette that is served with a vine-ripened tomato. It is literally a mouth-watering delight as his li hing mui pineapple chutney with foie gras is a treat of decadence. Malassadas, the egg-rich sugar-coated Portuguese fried doughnut, can be found rolled in li hing mui-spiked sugar. And who could deny that a margarita in a li hing mui-lined glass is positively delicious?

More combinations of traditional foods with new ingredients point to kim chee, the spicy, garlicky pickled cabbage of our Korean roots, paired with cream cheese for a dip. Hawaiian lomi salmon gets the same treatment, too. Chef Sam Choy created won tons filled with brie, the French semi-soft cheese with a rind, dipped in a pineapple marmalade. Mochi, traditional rice cakes of our Japanese heritage, traditionally filled with sweet azuki or lima beans, are now flavored with chocolate, coconut, pumpkin, sweet potato, butter, and even filled with peanut butter. And those malassadas, a defining treat of our plantation-era past, are infused today with chocolate or coffee cream, haupia and liliko'i curd.

Our fruits are used in ways never thought of before. Salsa, the Mexican and Spanish equivalent of sauce, is usually thought of as chopped tomatoes, onions, cilantro, garlic, and chili. In Hawai'i Regional Cuisine we make it with mango, pineapple, papaya, and other fresh fruits, accentuating their bright flavors with onions, cilantro, garlic, and chili. What fun.

Fried rice, once a dish you found in Chinese restaurants or something you threw together to use up leftovers, is now a fine dish that's served in white tablecloth restaurants, alongside, perhaps, some perfectly cooked pūlehu ribs or lusciously moist fried pork chops. The best fried rice is defined by the savory combination of bacon, SPAM, kamaboko, char siu, green onions, eggs, a dash of oyster sauce, and maybe a little kim chee.

Chinese-style steamed fish is a no-nonsense preparation of steaming fish with ginger (a traditional Chinese combination), then dousing it with hot oil and soy sauce and a generous handful of slivered green onions and chopped cilantro. It's what our immigrant forebears dined on; today it's been elevated to the status of haute cuisine, served in the finest dining rooms at eye-popping prices.

The list of ingredients, foods, and preparations used in new ways that permeate island cuisine today goes on and on. The important thing is that today's Hawai'i cuisine has not lost its flavor roots. Traditional dishes and flavors persist as testament to their heritage and to their good taste. We tweak these favorite foods in interesting and lively ways, elevating simple, humble foods to the status of gourmet, fine dining dishes. Ours is a constantly evolving cuisine, more delicious as we include the endless stream of influences that converge in our island state. No doubt, in another two decades, our food will have changed even more but will still hold on to our delicious tasty roots.

Joan Namkoong is a foodie and free-lance food writer. She has been writing about the Hawai'i food scene for over a dozen years and has been instrumental in the growth of farmers markets on O'ahu and the island of Hawai'i. She is the author of several books, including *Family Traditions in Hawai'i, Go Home, Cook Rice*, and most recently, *Food Lover's Guide to Honolulu.*

The Kim Chee Test

For En Suk

Joseph Stanton

It wasn't because
        I made your daughter happy,
        wore hair on all sides of my face,
        or voted for McGovern.

It was because on that day in 1972,
        in the only Korean restaurant in downtown LA,
        I passed what you called "the kim chee test."

My almost deft chopstick technique surprised you
        having no way of knowing
        that I had been practicing for weeks,
        trying to grasp
        even the greatest of difficulties —
        peas, peanuts, and Jell-O.

"Is he eating it?" you shouted
        from the opposite end of that long, low table.
"Yea, I think he likes it!"
        one of your friends shouted back.

Kim chee:
        the best of it sears the tongue like a battle cry
        a warm scream of pride
        at being alive
        and Korean.
        It's hotter stuff
        than I was born to handle,
        but the taste is there.

That red-orange, peppery incandescence
     of won bok and daikon
     rose to me then as it has so often since,
     spikes of terrible light inexorably dawning.

I swallowed hard,
     struggling not to gasp
     or lurch too quickly
     for the salving, golden remedy,
     foaming icy at the brim.

     Then I reflected:
          this beer comes from where I come from:
          the city of Cardinals, of mighty river meetings,
          of the world's largest croquet wicket.

     Congratulations to you,
          my Korean father,
          you chose the right brew,
          you just passed the Michelob test.

Joseph Stanton's books of poems are *A Field Guide to the Wildlife of Suburban O'ahu, Cardinal Points: Poems on St. Louis Cardinals Baseball, Imaginary Museum: Poems on Art,* and *What the Kite Thinks*. His nonfiction books include *The Important Books: Children's Picture Books as Art and Literature* and *Stan Musial: A Biography.* He has published in such journals as *Bamboo Ridge, Poetry, Harvard Review,* and *New York Quarterly*. He teaches Art History and American Studies at the University of Hawai'i at Mānoa.

Savoring the Flavors of Food and Art in Hawai'i

Victoria Gail-White

The Hawaiian Islands offer a unique art and food history — indeed, probably the most unique of any American state. Our location in the middle of the Pacific Ocean and the limitations and advantages of agriculture in a tropical climate have, for many years, dictated the foods we eat. For centuries, these same advantages and limitations have inspired artists to create works of art using our exotic foods as subject matter. More recently, they have inspired local chefs to create a unique cuisine that is artistically presented.

We have all seen a painting of food that has made us hungry. Our eyes and our appetites are connected. The eye plays an important part in the pleasure of eating as well as in the enjoyment of art. And color, essential to many works of art, has been found in medical research to be responsible for either suppressing appetite (blue) or bringing it about (red).

We tend to eat first with our eyes, so it is no wonder that our obsession with food is not only in the eating of it but also in the pleasures of painting and sculpting it.

What inspires artists

European and American artists who traveled to paradise in the 1800s sketched and painted the unusual visual delights they discovered here. Most of the nineteenth century artworks of edible fare in Hawai'i were beautiful realistic renditions, in various media (watercolor, oil on canvas, etchings, lithographs, bronze, and wood carvings), of breadfruit, mangos, pineapples, taro, guava, papayas, banana, macadamia nuts, lychee, coconut, limu, fish, and so forth.

These exotic foods are still popular inspirations for artists and sculptors today. You don't have to go very far to find fruit trees — many of them are in our own backyards. However, the styles for rendering our fruits and foodstuffs have changed enormously.

Abstracted as well as realistic art works depicting local foods can be found in most galleries and museums, on every

"Study of Hawaiian Fish" (oil on canvas) by Hubert Vos, 1898, from The Honolulu Academy of Arts collection.

Hawaiian Island, in a much larger variety of media to include clay, fiber, various printmaking techniques, photography, and glass. The foods we love to eat inspire us to express ourselves.

Paintings of how we catch and make the food we eat in Hawai'i can also be found in the nineteenth- and twentieth-century collections in the Bishop Museum and the Honolulu Academy of Arts. Hawaiian net fishermen perched on lava rocks, night fishermen with torches at the water's edge, fish ponds, hukilaus, taro patches and rice paddies, men pounding poi, hunters, pineapple and sugar cane workers, men climbing coconut trees, and the transport of foodstuffs via outrigger canoes distinguish the artistic representations of Hawaiian food and fasten an unmistakable sense of place to these artworks. They don't catch fish like that in Kansas!

American painter Hubert Vos's large oil on canvas, "Study of Hawaiian Fish" (1898), on display in the John Dominis & Patches Damon Holt Gallery at the Honolulu Academy of Arts, almost smells of the Pacific Ocean. We can virtually taste the beautiful flesh of these colorful, freshly caught local fish. In fact, it looks as though one might just slip out of the painting!

What inspires us to eat

The first impact of a satisfying meal is usually the way it is presented. The artistic presentation of serving food has undergone as much creative growth as the way we paint and sculpt it. I have always been of the opinion, having been a professional chef, that the culinary arts belong in the art departments of universities. Indeed, this art form is leaping and bounding in the same way the

Impressionists, the Fauvists, and the Abstract Impressionists did. Many plates of foods served in award-winning eating establishments in Hawai'i today are almost too beautiful to eat.

When did the artistic presentation of food become popular? The "subtlety," invented in the Middle Ages for grand occasions, was built from a mixture of edible and inedible ingredients. This large ornamental centerpiece was sculpted to represent objects and symbols meaningful to the guests of honor at a feast — in the same way that ice sculptures and wedding cakes are popular today.

In the early nineteenth century, around the same time that pineapple and coffee traveled to the Hawaiian Islands, France's Marie-Antoine Carême's decorative centerpieces reached their peak. Carême, known as "the cook of kings and the king of cooks," left behind artistic renditions of his Gothic towers, Indian Pavilions, Chinese pagodas, and Turkish fountains all sculpted out of foodstuffs, made chiefly of a pastry of almond paste, sugar, and colors that were a mind-boggling feast fantasy for the eyes. His creativity with food and the sculpting of it were artistic and innovative. The artistic and creative presentation of food became an issue that great European chefs built their reputations on. "A well displayed meal is enhanced 100 percent in my eyes," wrote Carême.

By contrast, the Hawaiian "Native Feast" photo from the 1870s shows a historic lū'au with particular attention paid to

"Native Feast" (photo) by C.A. Brown, 1870s, from the Hawai'i State Archives.

presentation. Here, it is not the surplus of simple foods that is impressive, but the artistic crafts of the woven lauhala mats for the ground cover and the carved wooden calabash bowls and trays made of monkey pod or koa wood for the serving of the food. The lū'au feast, much of which is cooked in an imu of embers, is a more casual affair than its European counterpart, and served outdoors surrounded by the natural beauty of the islands.

In America, in the 1950s and '60s, M.F.K. Fisher, Craig Claiborne, Julia Child, and James Beard gave cooking a sense of dignity and adventure — paying particular attention to the artistic and appetizing presentation of food on an everyday basis. The new combinations of food that arose from the cross-cultural population in Hawai'i, at that time, began to be an inspiration for a smorgasbord of colors and flavors. Hawai'i's cuisine was beginning to find its own taste as well as visual vocabulary inspired by much of the beauty of our island home.

Today, there is an "anything goes" attitude and competitiveness in the food industry that is mind-boggling. For the first time in the American history of food, there is a channel on television that is totally devoted to chefs, competition, and regional cuisines. Well-known Hawai'i-based chefs participate in these competitions regularly. The artistic presentation of the food they cook is always part of the criteria for a winning entry.

In 1991, after the rise of what came to be known as American Regional Cuisine, a group of a dozen Hawaiian chefs revolutionized our culinary world in the islands by creating Hawai'i Regional Cuisine. They have taken our local foodstuffs and turned them into deliciously edible works of art while at the same time supporting the local farmers and fishermen.

Hawai'i Regional chefs and their protégés have an international reputation because, like any artist, they pay particular attention to their canvas or paper — the plate, color, size, and shape are all taken into consideration. Their palette of colors — the foods they use — are also connected to the many flavors they wish to incorporate into the dish. Their style of plating, or painting their masterpiece, also takes into consideration food texture, taste, and the spatial and dimensional aspects of their creation. These chefs are not only painting a food picture, they are also painting a flavor experience with each addition of sauce or ingredient added to their creation.

The renowned architect, Frank Lloyd Wright, wrote, "Dining is and always was a great artistic opportunity." This is true in Hawai'i today.

For over thirty years, Kapi'olani Community College has been offering accredited courses in the culinary arts with attention to food presentation — taking into account that the first part of a memorable meal is experienced with our eyes.

Today, the multi-ethnic cuisine of the islands translates into the multi-creative presentations of this fusion cuisine. And these unique presentations, like the artist-chefs themselves, are what turn a restaurant into an edible art gallery. With different food focuses on different islands and the many galleries and museums that display the artists varied renderings of our local food bounty, what Hawai'i sees and eats today, and in the future, will always be a moveable feast.

Our three-dimensional wonderland inspires our expression. Seasonal and exotic foods moving from island to island, and new taste innovations given artistic consideration in presentation, give Hawai'i a unique signature in what has become the synthesis of both the artistic and culinary worlds.

Victoria Gail-White is a former gallery owner, fiber artist and teacher, Culinary Institute of America-trained chef, and has been writing art reviews for *The Honolulu Advertiser* since 2001.

Kaukau Time

I went to school there, ʻŌlaʻa. I get along with all the children. During that era, not much Filipinos. So, I usually mingle with Japanese boys, some Hawaiian boys. Well, they treat me as any one of them, you know. They not particular over this. When we go to school before, we used to bring what they call this "kaukau tin." Double-decker kind lunch can, small one. I get some friends, lunch time, they tell me, "Sabas, come eat." They share. Sometimes, when I bring plenty lunch, I share my food with them, too.

Sabas Jamito
(From the Oral History Project Kalihi: Place of Transition, *1984. Edited from an interview by Warren Nishimoto.)*

Unstill Life With Mangos

John Wythe White

[1]
One morning, reading the paper, she hears a mango fall. An abrupt snap of release, a rustling descent through thick leaves, a thud that sounds too heavy, a bounce, a settling in the underbrush. She walks outside to fetch it. The sun on her face feels strong for so early in the day. The ground is already warm.

Yellow and orange fruit, bright as flame. Before now, she has seen them only in Mexico, much smaller. This one's as big as a softball but oddly shaped, a roundness radiating from a flattened axis, "oblong" too ordinary a word for such an eccentric variation. Spheroid? Ellipsoid? Ovoid? It looks like a swollen comma.

A thick drop of sap oozes from the broken stem, leaving a shiny trail on the skin, sticky on her fingertips. Up in the tree is a spectacle of mass ripening, mangos in every phase of change, like maple leaves in autumn, turning from dark green to crimson to orange to banana-skin yellow. She remembers a maple tree a few blocks away from her childhood home. Whenever she mentions it, nobody believes her. No one can conceive of a maple tree in Los Angeles, an autumn in Southern California.

Mosquitoes attack her ankles, sending her back inside. Fortunately Hawaiian mosquitoes are small, leaving minor bites that stop itching after a few minutes. Their California counterparts raised lumps she would scratch for hours.

In the kitchen she rinses off the dirt, peels the skin, and eats the orange fruit down to the seed like corn off a cob, rotating it while chewing, leaning over the sink, juice dripping from her chin and fingers. It is the most accommodating fruit she has ever eaten, with no major obstacles on the path to gratification. Easy to peel, no fibers to pull off, no pulp or seeds to spit out, nothing to pick from between her teeth, only juicy, creamy fruit, sweeter than the ripest peach or plum.

She closes her hand over the flat-sided seed, template for the fully mature shape, the maximum swelling of flesh. This is the seed of the fruit from the tree in the yard of the cottage she lucked into, a complete but tiny house, further dwarfed by the mango tree, its branches partially covering one side of the roof. A bonsai house, well-kept, where she will remain in her recently reduced circumstances as long as the landlord allows. Forty-two, divorced, childless, adjusting to solitude, her old life has been cut away, all the people and places, and a new one grows from what's left. She knows it will not be the same, but she doesn't know how it's going to be different.

Her first mango, and one is all it takes. The rash appears within twenty-four hours, on the soft undersides of her wrists. Lumpy, unbearably itchy, it reminds her of poison oak — a curse she thought she'd left behind. Scratching makes it worse, possibly even spreads it, but not scratching is unthinkable. When it comes to poison oak (and whatever she's picked up now), she has no self control and wants none.

It crawls up her forearms. Before she wises up it's in the hollows of her ankles where she scratched the mosquito bites, and on her neck and forehead. On hot nights it spreads down her thighs in a red wave of swollen, sweating flesh. The itching leaves her sleepless and cranky. At work she is unable to concentrate. With people, impatient and distracted. Alone at home, sorry for her miserable self.

She suffers for a week while the poison runs its course. In feverish darkness, she ponders her complicity in visiting such a plague on her body. If there are no accidents, which she believes is true at some level of consciousness, then why did she do this to herself? If there is a God, then what sin has she committed to deserve such a punishment? Is this a down payment on the price of paradise?

Unlike the apple of Eden, the mango of Kaimukī presents an opportunity to keep on sinning long after the last bite has been consumed. The mango's deepest, most irresistible temptation is not to eat but to scratch. Without hesitation she will yield. For a minute's relief in the here and now, she will willingly trade hours of future torment. She scratches her skin until it bleeds.

In the yard, mangos fall. Three or four a day, more overnight. She leaves them all to rot. She walks among her fallen, decaying crop, savoring her obstinate refusal to harvest. The air is black with fruit flies. Cockroaches the size of toy cars join worms and beetles at the sweet feast. Up in the trees, birds raise a ruckus while pecking holes in the ripening fruit. Over the fence, from her neighbors' yard, an ingenious apparatus appears and hovers in the branches, a long bamboo stalk with a wire-rimmed canvas pocket at the end, big enough to hold two or three mangos, designed to pluck them before they fall and pull them away to more eager, most likely rash-immune, arms. Rape of the mangos. Sole eyewitness declines to notify authorities.

Raw, itchy, angry, she refuses to touch another mango. Coated with a flaking crust of calamine and scabrous flesh, she stays inside. She has not been expelled from the garden, she's boycotting it. She's on strike against God.

[2]

A year later she's back on the job, this time with a better attitude. Armed with information and the proper tools. She has questioned her neighbors and friends at work. Searched the Kaimukī library. Queried the 'Net. Learned her lessons.

It turns out the mango *is* related to poison oak. The irony does not escape. The house she last lived in was at the edge of a wood she rarely entered for fear of poison oak. Inches off the trails, easy to spot but hard to avoid, it grew everywhere in Portola Valley, a dangerous bush proliferating beneath live oak and bay laurel trees for miles at a stretch.

Even if she managed to prevent the leaves from touching her skin, she would invariably pick up the oil from her clothing or the fur of her dog. She always had a run of the rash somewhere on her body, but she never learned to live with it. She heard that as Portola led his troops over the Santa Cruz mountains way back when, some burned the shrub in their campfires, inhaled the poison, and died horrible deaths.

She learns that her tree is not a "Haden" or "Pirie" (two local favorites) but a hybrid which, by an act of genetic serendipity, produces fruit as desirable as that of either variety.

She figures it's the sap that gave her the rash, that she's not allergic to the leaves of the tree, the pollen from the flowers, or the skin or meat of the ripe fruit. Blisters did not bloom on her lips after she ate it. All she needs to do, she is certain, is avoid touching the sap.

Thus her outfit: Tennis shoes. Old blue jeans tucked into the tops of white athletic socks. Heavy-duty rubber gloves pulled over the cuffs of a long-sleeved denim work shirt. Red bandanna rolled and worn as a sweat band around her forehead. Exposed skin on face and neck covered with mosquito repellent. Baseball cap.

Her tools: An aluminum ladder to get her up on the roof, where she has access to the upper branches of the tree, and a homemade mango-picker modeled after her neighbors' stealth grabber. Getting the bamboo was not easy. The commercial fishing-rod poles weren't long enough. She ended up cutting her own, a twelve-foot stalk, in a bamboo forest on Mount Tantalus, strictly legal, with a permit from the Forestry Division to show on demand.

She's outfitted, armed, and ready to go.

The harvest never comes.

Mango trees are supposed to fruit between March and October, but on hers nothing happens. Months pass, red new leaves turn to green, flowers bloom, and pollen dusts the air, but no buds show. She asks her neighbors, what's the problem? They say, it happens. You never know, sometimes a mango tree skips a year or two.

[3]

In year three, the early signs are favorable. In January, tiny green buds appear in the tree. She goes up on the roof to get a closer look. She can't imagine what she'll do with all these mangos. There must be hundreds of them.

Early in February, the trade winds rise. They blow day and night, pummeling her thin-walled house, relentlessly clanging the neighbors' wind chimes, flapping loose gates, rolling wayward trash cans down the street, jarring the local dog network into barking fits. One night, awake after a chaotic, wind-driven dream, she hears a small object hit the roof, roll down the slope and plunge into silence.

It's not until the next night, after hearing it repeated several times, that she realizes what's making the sound. The winds are blowing the budding mangos off the tree.

The next morning she sees them scattered all over the yard. Climbs to the roof and finds more in the rain gutter. Perfect, comma-shaped miniatures the size of golf balls. She is definitely losing her mangos. At this rate, she calculates with a rush of panic, they will soon be totally gone. She feels like a woman going bald.

In the same way she used to worry about her failed marriage, she wonders if it's her fault. Are the young mangos unable to withstand the winds because she didn't water the tree enough? Because she watered too much? Should she have, as one neighbor suggested, fed the tree some fertilizer? Is there some elixir she doesn't know about, available from an obscure garden supplier, that toughens up mango stems the way gelatin fortifies fingernails? Back in India, home of the mango, is some prayer or ritual act performed during a significant phase of the tree's annual cycle?

By day, in frustration, she rakes up the fallen embryos. At night she cringes at the terrible falling sounds. But she can't stop the process. The winds blow for weeks, and finally she concedes. This year there will be no harvest. And this year is her last chance. Uncomfortable as a talker-to-plants, she decides to write the tree a letter. She composes it on the computer, then handwrites the final draft. It is an apology (*O mango, abundantly leafy yet fruitless, forgive me if I have inadvertently or neglectfully done you harm*), a farewell (*For I am out of here, as the house has been sold and I have been notified to vacate the premises in sixty days*) and a warning:

I gravely urge you to prepare for a shock far worse than the still-gusting Cruel Winds of February. The landlord tells me that your new owners intend to prune you in a most extreme manner, reducing your farthest-reaching branches to mere stubs, sparing only your life, allowing you to grow back but never again to such house- and yard-dwarfing proportions.

She addresses the envelope "MANGO" and delivers the letter personally, affixing it to the tree's trunk with a push pin. She stores the stepladder under the house, rakes up the fallen buds a final time, and turns her attention from the tree.

She spends less time at home, leaving for work an hour earlier each morning to give herself free time for afternoon house-hunting. The effort is discouraging. She soon gives up looking only for a house with a mango tree in the yard, admits it's asking too much. But she stands firm on her refusal to live in a high-rise.

Weeks pass. A month before moving day, she is no closer to finding a new home. The winds fall. Calm is restored to the neighborhood and her dreams. On a sunny morning in mid-March, she hears a familiar sound. It can't be, but it sounds like a mango falling. She goes outside to check.

She finds the newly fallen fruit among several others in various stages of consumption and decay. Above, the tree is filled with ripening mangos. How could this be happening? She watched this season's mangos die an early death. Are these new ones or buds she failed to notice that escaped the winds? It doesn't matter. She has thirty days to reap the harvest.

[4]

For the next month, mangos are her life. Gathering, processing, and distribution take hours a day. Every morning before work, every evening before dinner, she's busy with mangos. She can't skip a day. There's gold in the yard, and she's compelled to mine it. Determined to make amends for prior neglect.

It becomes a ritual. First an Easter-egg hunt in the yard, a search for the bright-colored treasures concealed in the bushy green mondo grass and under the walking lily. She carries two plastic supermarket bags, one for keepers, one for throwaways. As long as she stays on top of the situation, most are keepers.

The trick is to get to the mangos before other creatures do. Some are goners already, deeply bruised or split open on impact, perforated by bird beaks, munched by insects, swarming with fruit flies. Some can be partially salvaged. At the height of the harvest she gathers a dozen mangos a day, just from the ground.

Up on the roof, it's a different drill: survey the tree, check on the crop, and selectively harvest. Walk along the diagonal rooftop, hand-picking the fruits or netting them. She takes only the brightest-colored mangos, ripe and ready to fall, their stems easily broken with a quick tug. Some mornings she comes down the ladder with fifteen or sixteen mangos, the bag so heavy its handholds stretch like taffy.

Still in uniform, she sets up the home processing plant. First she washes the mangos in warm, soapy water and rubs them with a sponge to remove the hardened sap. Next she rinses them and allocates each to one of three dish drainers, sorting by degree of ripeness for later distribution to the refrigerator, paper grocery bags, or production line.

The production line is the fate of fruit that can't wait. She peels the skin and cuts most of the meat off with a knife, then takes the seed in both rubbery hands and squeezes the rest into a big bowl. She puts equal portions of slices and mash into sealable sandwich bags and transfers them to the freezer where, she has been assured, they will last for at least six months.

Every day, she eats what she can — mangos straight, sliced mangos with granola and milk, mangos blended into smoothies with banana, papaya, and yogurt. Still, she has hundreds more than she can ever use. Bagged by the dozen, she gives them away to neighbors, friends, people at work, the landlord, the new owners when they come by to see the house. In return, some bring her mango bread, mango jam, mango chutney, pickled mango, mango ice cream.

She keeps a mango count, enters it into her computer and views the data on pie charts and bar graphs. At the end of the harvest, she has collected four hundred-forty mangos — an average of twenty mangos a day for a period of twenty-two days, not counting the throwaways, only two every three days. Her freezer is filled with orange baggies, room for nothing else. One shelf of her refrigerator is still occupied by ripening mangos, down from three at the peak of the harvest. Finally the tree is empty.

The night before she leaves, she writes a farewell letter:

Dear Mango:

I and others too numerous to name would like to thank you for your abundance. Your progeny were well received by all.

I have good news. The new owners, impressed by the quality of your fruit (as personally experienced) and the extent of your seasonal yield (as witnessed in my computer-assisted presentation), have decided to abandon their radical chainsaw agenda for your future. Instead, you will be trimmed only minimally, to bring your branches away from the roof and telephone lines.

I leave you in what I now believe to be good hands.
Aloha.

Her new home has no mango tree. What it has is lychee, avocado, kukui, and a big patch of banana plants.

John Wythe White's short stories, articles, essays, travel writing, journalism, theater reviews, and humor have been published for many years in Hawai'i-based magazines and newspapers. He has published a collection of stories, *Short-Timers in Paradise*, and a novel, *A High and Beautiful Wave.*

Ono Crack Seed

© 1983 G.KAGIMOTO

SWEET LI HING MUI   SOFT LI HING MUI   BABY LI HING MUI
SWEET SOUR LI HING MUI   SEEDLESS LI HING MUI   WET
LI HING MUI   SALTY SEED   WET SALTY SEED   ROCK SALT
PLUM   SWEET SOUR SEEDLESS PLUM   KAM CHOW HAM
MUI BULLDOG SEED RED CUTTLEFISH LEGS   BABY SEED
SWEET SOUR WHOLE SEED DRIED CRACK SEED   SAKURA
ARARE SOFT IKA CHILI SMOKED OCTOPUS ISO PEANUTS

CANE HAUL ROAD LTD., HAWAII

The Vietnamese New Year, a Time of Symbolism, Celebration, and Plenty

Betty Shimabukuro

To do it right, you must cook early and cook a lot. Once the Lunar New Year begins, the household must be ready.

It is time for Tet, the most important of holidays among Vietnamese. It is time for *banh chung* and *banh day,* or sticky rice cakes wrapped in banana leaves; of the hearty pork stew with boiled eggs called *thit kho;* of stuffed bittermelon, candied fruits, and special offerings such as papaya and soursop, valued for their symbolism.

In Vietnam, where luxuries are hard-won and work is constant, *Tet Nguyen Dan,* the Lunar New Year Festival, is the one time of leisure and excess, a time to spend on costly foods, new clothes, and other trappings of spring.

"In Vietnam people work for a whole year for Tet," says Xuan-Mai Pavey, owner of the new Garden of Saigon restaurant in Chinatown. "For the first three days, everybody has parties, everybody has food in the house."

To fulfill the traditions requires an investment of time as well as money, the idea being to be ready for New Year visitors, to feed the family for several days, to meet obligations to ancestors' spirits and the household gods.

Best example would be the sticky rice cakes made one or two weeks before the new year, dozens at a time. Traditionally, they were steamed outdoors, the entire family in attendance to feed the fire and keep water in the pot. "You cook all night long," recalls Thanh Lo Sananikone, originally from Hue in central Vietnam. "Family, friends, and relatives sit there and watch because you have to add water all night."

In her kitchen here, Sananikone maintains the tradition on her stovetop, where she'll make twenty-five or thirty cakes for gifts and to serve visitors. "It takes all Saturday and the evening and the night," she says. "Usually I start too late and I have to cook overnight. I have to get up three times."

Why all the bother? Because of King Hung-vuong, father of many sons, who decided to give his throne to the one who could bring him the most meaningful dish of food. The sons hunted, fished, brought back all manner of delicacies, but it was the youngest son, Tiet-Lieu, who won the kingdom. His gift of glutinous rice steamed into cakes deemed most significant because in their simplicity they honored the basic foodstuff of the people.

Tong Ma remembers Tet during his childhood in southern Vietnam as the one time he was given new clothes. He remembers a betting game played with dice marked with animal figures; collecting red-wrapped packets of money from his parents' friends; candied fruits, or *mut* — especially the ginger, coconut, carrot, and the rare lotus root and lotus seed.

In the old days the celebrating lasted ten days, but now it is more likely to be a three-day break from work and school, Ma says. The candies were kept on hand to offer visitors who came and went throughout this time. "You sit down and eat this and drink tea and talk story."

Also essential: a collection of symbolic fruits. Here is where traditions vary some. Ma values mango, papaya, coconut, and soursop. Chau Tran, a native of Saigon (now Ho Chi Minh City), would add oranges, pomelo, and pineapple and subtract coconut as too common. "People save all year," Tran says, "for Tet, people want something expensive."

The symbolism in some cases is a matter of wordplay: *Du-du* is the word for papaya; *du* in itself means "enough." *Xoai,* for mango, means "plentiful." *Mang cau* means soursop; *cau* is "to pray." To have these fruits in the home is to pray that your family will have enough in the new year.

Oranges are valued for their lucky color, pineapples for their perfume. "People believe that when you have all these things all together they will bring you good things for all the year," Tran says.

Watermelon, in season in Vietnam at the new year, is the chosen dessert, she adds. "In every household you have to choose the biggest one. And the redder it is inside, the better luck you'll have."

Roasted watermelon seeds are a favorite snack, Sananikone says. "The mouth becomes red when you eat them. Young girls like to eat this because they aren't allowed to have lipstick yet."

The twenty-third day of the twelfth month of the lunar year is Le Tao Quan, Feast of the Household Gods. On this day families pray to the guardian spirit of the kitchen and make offerings of rice cakes and fruit. The kitchen god then goes to heaven to report on the family's behavior for the year, and a new god is assigned to look after the family in the year to come.

On the thirtieth day, prayers are said at the family altar to invite the ancestors to help close out the old year. Offerings are placed outside the home in honor of "wandering souls," people without homes, Sananikone says.

In the homes of many transplanted Vietnamese, these traditions remain strong, to the point that even the labor-intensive rice cakes are fixed at home, not purchased.

Sananikone has been away from her homeland since 1975 and remains mindful of the rituals of Tet. Her two grown children live in San Francisco and New York, but she mails them their homemade rice cakes each year. "I hope they keep the traditions."

Recipes: Two traditional dishes of Tet

Thanh Lo Sananikone makes *thit kho*, a stew of pork, hard-boiled eggs, and coconut juice, to last through Tet.

By tradition, family and friends may visit at any time. "If they come at eleven o'clock, you eat lunch; if they come at five, you eat dinner," Sananikone says. A dish like this serves everyone for a long time.

The flavor improves, she says, as the dish ages. Pickled vegetables are a traditional side dish served with the sticky rice cakes and other new year foods. These are adaptations of Sananikone's recipes:

Thit Kho
Vietnamese New Year's Stew

2 tablespoons sugar
1 pound pork butt, in 1-inch cubes
2 teaspoons fish sauce
1/4 teaspoon salt
1/4 teaspoon pepper
2 cloves garlic, peeled
1/2 cup coconut juice (water from fresh coconut)
4 hard-boiled eggs, peeled

Melt sugar over low heat, cooking until caramelized and slightly brown. Stir in pork butt in cubes; brown.

Stir in fish sauce, salt, pepper, garlic, and coconut juice. Add eggs and water as needed to cover. Bring to a boil, then simmer until meat is cooked through and eggs turn brown. Taste and adjust seasonings.

Optional: Add cabbage if there is enough liquid. Serves 4.

Dua Mon
Vegetables in Fish Sauce

— Dried vegetables:
2 carrots
1 green papaya or 1 turnip
12 shallots, peeled
12 garlic cloves, peeled
12 small red chile peppers

— Sauce:
3/4 cup plus 2 tablespoons nuoc mom (Vietnamese fish sauce)
1/4 cup plus 1 tablespoon sugar
1-1/2 cups water

Peel carrots. Peel and seed papaya or peel turnip. Cut into 1-1/2-inch sticks (may also be cut into shapes of flowers). Dry vegetables in dehydrator, following manufacturer's directions, or in the oven: Rub 1 tablespoon salt into vegetables; let stand 30 minutes, then rinse, squeeze and pat dry. Dry in a 200-degree oven for 2 hours, turning every 30 minutes.

To make sauce: Heat fish sauce and add sugar; stir until melted. Add water and boil 2 minutes; cool.

Layer vegetables in a 1-quart jar. Pour sauce into jar. Marinate at least 2 weeks.

Variation: Dried pineapple pieces may also be added.

Holiday foods

— Cakes made of glutinous rice are essential to Tet. Round cakes represent the universe; square cakes represent Earth.

— Candied fruits and vegetables — carrots, coconut slices, ginger lotus root, and lotus seeds — are served with tea, as is traditional in China as well.

Seasonal symbolism

Certain fruits are valued for their color, scent, or because their names have double meanings.

— Soursop, for example, is called *mang cau. Cau* by itself means 'to pray.'

— Words for mango and papaya can also mean 'plentiful' and 'enough.'

— Roasted watermelon seeds are valued for their red color, considered lucky.

Betty Shimabukuro is editor of the features section of the *Honolulu Star-Bulletin* and is also the paper's main food writer. She is also the author of the cookbook *By Request*, and co-author of *What Hawai'i Likes to Eat.* This article was first printed in the *Honolulu Star-Bulletin* on February 2, 2000.

The Saimin Lady

Was a saimin noodle soup lady that in the evening, when the working people would come home, she had one of these red wagons pulled by hand. Those wagons came from Japan. Two big wheels, little lattice-work. In the inside of it would be two big pots of hot water. There'd be charcoal underneath burning to keep it hot. On the side of this little wagon, she would have her eggs all chopped up, meat, shoyu, whatever ingredients she needed was right there.

From the time she entered into our lane, the smell of the soup broth tells you the saimin lady is at the entrance, now get your money ready. Ten cents for one big saimin bowl. So you divide your ten cents bowl with another kid. Half and a half. Fifty cents would feed this big family of ten for saimin. Then you have the barbecue stick. Five cents, one. With three meats on top. The smell would be so strong, and so nice that you cannot let the saimin lady pass. You go to go look for ten cents! Even if meant tomorrow you going starve, you look for that ten cents.

Eleanor Wilson Heavey
(From Hanahana: An Oral History Anthology of Hawai'i's Working People. *Interviewed by Perry Nakayama.)*

hardly any
char siu nowdays

Chewing the Fat

David K. Choo

There used to be a food cart parked near the 'Ewa corner of Bishop and King streets in downtown Honolulu. If I had peered out of my cubicle, I could probably have seen the cart from my office window, four floors up, but I never bothered.

I also didn't bother to stop by and sample the vendor's food (empanadas, I think) as I rushed out of the office for lunch, usually to visit one of the same three or four eateries. Everyone else seemed to be doing the same, as the poor guy just smiled and nodded as we passed by in a blur. All of us worker bees were too busy to stop and try something new.

After several weeks, the food cart moved across the street to Tamarind Square, where there were larger crowds. However, they walked by just as fast. I haven't seen the food cart for weeks now. I think it's moved on to another corner somewhere.

A year ago, I would have spotted the empanada man as soon as he set up shop. I would have sampled every one of his meat pies, and I would have chatted with him, asking about his food, where he was from, getting his life's story in a five-minute conversation.

A year ago, I was an outgoing and daring urban explorer, seeking out the new and exciting, unusual and mundane. I was a food critic, and set out two or three days a week to taste Honolulu's fast and affordable lunchtime food, usually at hole-in-the-wall establishments run by people like the empanada man. I wrote a weekly dining column called "Choo on This" for the *Downtown Planet*, a free weekly newspaper distributed throughout metro Honolulu, from Kalihi to Kaimukī.

I wrote "Choo on This" from May 2003 until July 2006, when the Planet was suddenly and unexpectedly shut down. I'll admit that the week after it closed, I breathed a little sigh of relief. It's not easy penning a weekly dining column fifty-two times a year, year after year. Most of the time you eat alone. All of the time, you write alone. But it didn't take long for me to miss "Choo on This." Sure, I missed all those free lunches, but even more I missed the slightly offbeat urban world that I would have never discovered otherwise. Most of all, I missed the person I became when I ate and wrote.

It's amazing how daring and outgoing you are when you have an assignment, a deadline, and an expense account. When your editor and readers are counting on you and someone else is paying, even if it's only a seven-dollar or eight-dollar tab, you order boldly and eat with purpose. When I visited a new place, I'd try the signature dish or a menu item that struck me as unusual and provocative. I rarely hesitated.

Once a co-worker told me about a tasty Vietnamese snail soup. She couldn't remember the name of the restaurant, but she knew it was on King Street in Chinatown. So at lunchtime, I hit the pavement and headed 'Ewa, reading menus taped to storefront windows along the way. When I found the 99 Coffee Shop and its *bun oc*, a spicy snail soup, I reveled in my *Amazing Race*-like ability to find an obscure food item. When my server informed me that they were out of snails, I was undaunted. I ordered *bun rieu*, a crab and tomato soup, which featured, among other things, fish cake, bean sprouts, fried tofu, cubed pig's blood, hot peppers, pig's feet, and, of course, tomatoes, and crab roe. I think I'm still digesting that meal.

Then, of course, there was *fugu*, the delectable and deadly blowfish, a delicacy in Japan, which I stumbled upon at Aki-No-No, a sleepy izakaya near the University of Hawai'i at Mānoa. As soon as I read the hiragana on the menu, I knew that I had to try the ultimate thrill food. I'm not sure what I was thinking, but I had taken my allergy medicine that morning, so I felt emboldened.

I later learned that the fugu had been processed in Japan and shipped frozen to Hawai'i, so eating it wasn't exactly a death-defying experience. But there was enough of a trace of the deadly neurotoxins in the fish to numb my throat and the insides of my mouth. For a moment, I was dining on the edge. (By the way, fugu tastes a little like chicken.)

Of course, not everything I ate was bizarre or thrilling. A majority of the food I tried was fairly conventional, much of it was delicious, but all of it was new — to me, at least.

I soon discovered that the most interesting aspect of my job was meeting the people who cooked the food. I'd have brief conversations with them after my meal, usually over the telephone, but sometimes across the counter. There was, for instance, Akira and Noriko Tanaka, a couple from Japan, who visited Hawai'i five times before opening their kushiage restaurant in Puck's Alley, near the university. Nearly everything they served was breaded, fried, and stuck to the end of a bamboo skewer.

I also met Adela Visitacion and her sister Edralyn Verona, who hastily opened their Fort Street Mall restaurant Dreamers Home Style Café on their deceased father's birthday. It had always been his dream to run a restaurant. Several doors down is Angelo Hernandez, a native of Oakland, California, who paid a similar tribute to his dad with La Taqueria de Ramiro. The lunch counter serves some of the fattest and tastiest burritos in town.

And I'll never forget Vincent Kwon, a recovering ice addict, who was wandering the streets just a few years ago. With the help of family and friends and an unwavering belief in God, he was able to clean himself up and eventually open Grindz Restaurant. Like Kwon, several of the staff were homeless and recovering meth addicts. The food was warm and comforting, the service even more so. I watched Kwon's team work with vigor and pride, as if their lives depended on it.

Not long ago, I asked a successful and well-known kama'āina business executive the most important lesson he had learned doing business in Hawai'i.

"Never take more than you give," he said emphatically.

He then told me about working in the Wahiawā pineapple fields when he was a teenager, describing the hot, backbreaking work and the lunch breaks that never came too soon. The work crew — Japanese, Korean, Filipino, Hawaiian, and him, a *haole* kid — would sit in a circle and put their kaukau tins (lunch boxes) in the middle, sharing their food.

"One day, I ate the softest, most tender teriyaki I'd ever tasted," he said. "I asked, 'What is this? It's delicious.' Everyone laughed. It turned out to be dog. But it really was good."

That's what was beautiful about Hawai'i. We used to sit down together, eat each other's food and talk. We don't do that anymore. I know I don't. With a wife, a young son, and what will likely be a very old mortgage, I live according to schedules, budgets, and travel to and from work in straight lines. I miss being curious, wandering Honolulu with an empty stomach and a full notepad. Now I eat at too many theme restaurants and order too many combo meals.

The other day, I peered out my office window, looking for the food cart. It's long gone now. I wish I had taken the time to try one of those empanadas when I had a chance. I bet they were delicious — or, at least, interesting.

David K. Choo is the author of the book *Lunch Break Honolulu: 65 Great Places to Beat the Clock*, a collection of his dining reviews published this year by Watermark Publishing. This article first appeared in *Spirit of Aloha* magazine.

Chinese Hot Pot

Wing Tek Lum

My dream of America
is like *dá bìn lòuh*
with people of all persuasions and tastes
sitting down around a common pot
chopsticks and basket scoops here and there
some cooking squid and others beef
some tofu or watercress
all in one broth
like a stew that really isn't
as each one chooses what he wishes to eat
only that the pot and fire are shared
along with the good company
and the sweet soup
spooned out at the end of the meal.

Wing Tek Lum is a Honolulu businessman and poet. "Chinese Hot Pot" appears in his first collection of poetry, *Expounding the Doubtful Points*, published by Bamboo Ridge Press in 1987.

About the Cover and Art Work

The art work which appears on the cover of *We Go Eat: A Mixed Plate From Hawai'i's Food Culture* and throughout the pages of this anthology are the designs of Grant Kagimoto.

Kagimoto started Cane Haul Road, Ltd., in 1977, in a small cottage in Kaimuki. His designs — produced mostly for a highly successful line of screen-printed T-shirts — best reflect "an effort to preserve, spotlight, and celebrate Hawai'i's unique lifestyle."

This lifestyle — influenced by a large number of immigrant sugar plantation workers, blending Asian, European, Hawaiian, and American cultures — has provided a rich environment for Cane Haul Road's distinctive and original designs.

The term "mixed plate" has been used throughout this anthology. It appropriately describes the diversity of Cane Haul Road designs, which celebrate local (pidgin) English, multi-ethnic foods, customs, holidays, dress, plants. and animals — all captured with a sense of humor and playful reverence.

"As Hawai'i continues to be impacted by globalization," says Kagimoto, "we feel it is our mission to try and reflect those qualities that made our childhood and our present lives so special."

© 1982 G.Kagimoto